For God and Country

For God and Country:

Butler's 1944 Education Act

By

Elizabeth "Libi" Sundermann

Cambridge
Scholars
Publishing

For God and Country: Butler's 1944 Education Act

By Elizabeth "Libi" Sundermann

This book first published 2015

Cambridge Scholars Publishing

Lady Stephenson Library, Newcastle upon Tyne, NE6 2PA, UK

British Library Cataloguing in Publication Data
A catalogue record for this book is available from the British Library

ISBN (10): 1-4438-8383-2
ISBN (13): 978-1-4438-8383-2

To Dr. James E. Hayes, professor of education and grandfather

CONTENTS

PREFACE

This study, by a twenty-first century American of left-wing and atheist beliefs, attempts to continue to help rescue interwar and 1940s-era English Christian intellectuals and Conservative politicians from a "condescension" of history [of education]. As a historical study, it attempts to understand how and why educational philosophies were formed, and how and why education policies were enacted, without trying to judge the educational or pedagogical values or results of education policies and philosophies. As a historian rather than an educationalist, I wrote this book as an intellectual history, rather than a history of education. That said, having been raised by an extended family of left-wing American educators, I came to this work with a firm belief in the benefits of a liberal education and with criticisms of my own country's systems and policy decisions.

I began my work pouring over the pages of Brian Simon's important studies on English education. My research and subsequent analysis, however, forced me to make a fundamental shift in thinking. A consequent tight focus on Minister of Education R. A. Butler and his intellectual colleagues, particularly Conservative and Christian activists, dashed my Generation X and (naïve) liberal assumptions that these men and women were little more than die-hard Tories and antecedents of Thatcherism or the Christian-Right. Rather, Butler and his educationalist peers emerged as deeply complex men and women who weighed and measured social *and* cultural concerns and tradition *and* progress to create policy they believed could restore a viable Christian-civic humanism to England. I was—ironically—fortunate that I began this study after 9/11 and 7/7 when scholarly ideas about religion in England (and the United States) changed quickly to embrace interpretations of postsecularism. Perhaps this, and my identity as a Gen X American, led to my initial astonishment to find that Religious Education had been *mandated* by the 1944 Education Act in England.[1] This seemed incongruous in what was supposed to have been a secularizing century. I came to agree with other thinkers that the history of Religious Education, particularly after this mandate, had not just been—in

[1] Although formally "an Act to reform the law relating to education in England and Wales" this study's focus is on England.

many cases—under-analyzed, but in some cases almost systematically ignored.

My continued research and analysis led me to agree with other scholars that radical protagonists of the left, as well as those on the right, had contributed to the on-going partisan debates in English educational politics by misrepresenting, or at least misunderstanding, aspects of past policy decisions. A continued lack of self-awareness and introspection by both sides of the political spectrum contributed to the on-going confusion that stymied England's educational philosophies after 1944. Both the left and the right tried, in vain, to continue to reform English education. These controversies contained, paradoxically, bipartisan elitist attitudes toward education, vocation, and society that plagued late-twentieth century England. Yet I believed there must have been attempts to systematically bridge the divides and to create a national education system for all. I found this in my study of the making of the 1944 Act.

A 1984 sociological explanation of "educational policy and ideology" by Open University instructors argues that postwar educational policy was based on two widely accepted "axioms:" "(A) That universal education provided by the state could bring about peaceful social change and ameliorate at least some of the harsher injustices created by a class-divided society [and] (B) that an educated workforce was a prerequisite for economic growth" (section 2.2). In my reading, these goals clearly reflected proposals made by Butler and his intellectual colleagues for Religious Education and secondary and further education embedded in the Act. Why then, did partisan conflicts continue after the landmark 1944 Act? Parts of the answer are that some interpretations of the 1944 Act neglected to fully examine schemes for Religious Education, alternate forms of secondary education outside comprehensives, and further education—as well as non-governmental documents and discussions that are now seen as influencing the Act's legislation and spirit. Historians in the twentieth-century had left out parts of the story of the 1944 Act. This is natural as historiographical trends change and, fortunately, left room for new scholars to enter the historical discussions.

Scholars had noted that the rise of the professional classes in the nineteenth and twentieth centuries included an almost complete absorption of educational and intellectual status into a form of property. Harold Perkin, among others, traces the rise of the professional classes and the socio-cultural splintering that occurred between middle-class industrialists and middle-class intellectuals who rose up in society by dint of accumulation of material or intellectual capital. Working-class life, both in terms of careers and cultures, remained marginalized and degraded. The

English middle classes held to an ideal of freedom to work but only middle-class careers were considered independent. Professional vocations held by formally-educated men (and later women) that involved expensive or accredited education and training were regarded as having increased social or cultural value. Work that involved practical education and material production outside of formal higher education remained largely denigrated. The continued development and integration of mass culture and mass education contributed to a culture where educational credentials and financial compensation meant more than intellectualism and social welfare. Katharyne Mitchell calls this movement a form of "strategic cosmopolitanism" for privileged professional classes (2003). Perkin describes it as "self-destructive greed and corruption among professional elites" "who control the flow of income [and power] to steer more and more of it to themselves" (1996, abstract, xiv). In the late twentieth century both the left and the right continued construction on this educational-industrial complex of higher education which in turn shaped secondary education's structures and goals—often for the worse.

English education became focused on a battle for rights to formal further—higher—education. Politicians and educationalists thus lost focus on creating a viable educational philosophy for all that could benefit state welfare and the commonweal. Labour *and* Conservatives submerged ideas that education *and* training were necessary and vital parts of every citizen's life. These battles for formal education continue, and current educational policy reports suggest that no side has won but that English educational philosophies continue to suffer.

A theme of the 1944 Act, in my interpretation, was the maintenance of and renewed respect for spheres of society outside the ranks of professional society, where men, women, and children had a way forward that was not based on increased professionalization and material wealth, but on a philosophy of life-long learning and a sense of education as related to Christian-civic humanism. This was a program to open, not limit, the paths all citizens—regardless of birth—could chose, constrained only by a consideration of the commonweal and the individual's own interests and abilities. In order to do so, as Butler and his colleagues argued, educational philosophy must look toward diverse educational schemes tempered by social cohesion. Social cohesion, it was believed, could exist while educating citizens for the wide variety of occupations necessary in an industrialized society. A national faith—Christianity—would propagate mutual respect and commonweal spirit. Although I personally do not believe in the need for a *Christian*-based Religious Education in the national school system, philosophies of education for the welfare of the general public, rather than wedded to elitist ideals of a liberal education as the only way forward, still seem like a good idea—on both sides of the Atlantic.[2]

This preface would not be complete without some acknowledgements. Thanks to my family, friends, and students. You know who you are and how you helped. Thank you to my mentors and colleagues at the University of California, Davis, University of Washington, Tacoma and elsewhere. This book would not have been possible without you. Joanne Clarke Dillman, thank you, especially, for your encouragement and friendship. Special thanks to the School of Interdisciplinary Arts and Sciences at the University of Washington, Tacoma for awarding me a Research & Teaching Fund Award to support revision of an earlier draft of this work and to hire Jennifer Joyner—history B.A., MAIS candidate, writer, and friend—to proofread and make clever editing suggestions for the manuscript. Thanks Jen!

Finally, a few notes on the text: written by an American this book uses American English spelling in the main text but British English spelling in quotations and elsewhere as appropriate. A brief glossary of people and terms that may not be familiar to American or lay audiences is provided. I also made the decision to use an author-date system of notes and references for this book. This style is one with growing—but not full—acceptance by historians. The author-date style, to my mind, is less cumbersome for the reader and allows for a slimmer volume—both are important trends in our current age. I have strived, however, to provide readers with a clear guide to sources and materials used as well as limited footnotes for explanatory comments outside the main text. Any errors that remain in the text are my own.

---

[2] As a historian, I do believe we should teach for understanding of human spirituality in all its forms and practices.

INTRODUCTION

> The first duty that every generation owes to its children is to make its country and theirs safe and solvent. That is the precondition of all social reform.
> —R. A. Butler, "The 1944 Act Seen against the Pattern of the Times," 1952

Since its inception in England, scholars have provided clear interpretations for the 1944 Education Act's socio-educational legacy. From a historical point of view, however, the 1944 Act's Conservative and Christian cultural and intellectual backgrounds have been less clear. This book attempts to fill some of these gaps by analyzing the political, socio-cultural, and intellectual ideas the 1944 Act's architects, specifically Richard Austen (R. A.) Butler, President of the Board of Education, educationalist Fred Clarke, and sociologist Karl Mannheim, applied in crafting educational literature and legislation during the interwar and World War II periods. This focus on ideology, as well as a periodization that examines the 1944 Act's intellectual background and its legislation, reveals a philosophy, identified in this book as Christian-civic humanism, which borrowed from English intellectual and cultural history, but crafted a specific response to trends and problems in twentieth-century England.

In his memoirs Butler recalled,

> [Prime Minister] Churchill's [1941] Minute [forbidding initiation of education reform] was quite definite . . . [but] having viewed the milk and honey from the top of Pisgah, I was damned if I was going to die in the land of Moab . . . I decided to disregard what he said and go straight ahead [with education reform] . . . I intended to have an Education Bill, and three years [later] I placed such a Bill on the Statute Book" (1971, 95).

Three interpretations are drawn from this statement. First, Butler profoundly believed he could and *would* create legislation, despite any political barriers. Second and third, Butler had a plan for the 1944 Act before official reform efforts began and that scheme was envisioned as a spiritual crusade. This analysis suggests re-reading intellectual proposals, legislative policy, and supporting literature of the 1944 Act through postsecular lenses is necessary. As the Office for Standards in Education, UK (Ofsted) report "Making Sense of Religion" suggested in 2007, "debates about the relationship between religion and British identity have given a new impetus and urgency to the subject [of Religious Education in schools]." The postsecular analysis in this study reveals that Butler and his colleagues' visions for new educational legislation included not only the hot button issues of secondary and further education reforms but synchronized them with plans for a Religious Education that would bolster civic and spiritual development for English culture. The relationships between secondary and further education and Religious Education formed the basis for Butler's 1944 Act and his visions for British identity.

Although this study focuses on aspects of Butler's, Clarke's, and Mannheim's specific contributions to the intellectual and educational proposals of the 1944 Act, it also reaffirms a web of formal and informal collaborations by Christian intellectuals, educationalists, and Conservative social reformers who contributed to Christian-civic thought for educational reform in the 1930s and 1940s. These groups, with ties to Butler, Clarke and Mannheim, included the Moot, the All-Souls Group, the Conservative Committee on Postwar Problems, and the *Christian New-Letter*. Christian values and a transcendence of class and vocational conflicts through secondary and further education were widely regarded as symbiotic responses to international and domestic trends that threatened English society. Butler's practical efforts to [re]-build infrastructure, industry, and the English national economy and to re-stimulate Anglo-Christian values were embedded in two sections of the 1944 Act: "Religious Education in County and Voluntary Schools," (sections 25-30)—the historic mandate of religious instruction—and "Further Education," (sections 41-47). Special attention will be given to these sections of the 1944 Act in this study.

While there is little contention among scholars that the making of the 1944 Act was an important venture and its legislation a fundamental event in English educational history, its Christian-civic elements were submerged in the historical record after its passage. In part, this was a postwar reaction to its synthesis of patriotism through spirituality, commonweal, and education seen as reactionary, and thus inconsequential, to postwar narratives. It was also a natural result in the shift in principles and power from the wartime coalition government to the 1945 Labour government—although while after 1945 Butler remained a prominent Conservative politician, he no longer served in Education and while his 1944 Act stood, his influence and interpretations did not.

To some extent, the political change-over re-focused the meanings and implementation of the 1944 Act in post-World War II on a secular (and Labour) platform for secondary education for all. While this study does not provide a counterfactual, it does suggest that what Butler's 1944 Act proposed was not entirely what politicians and educationalists implemented. Although scores of historians—from renowned historian of education Brian Simon (1991) to renowned intellectual historian Jose Harris (2003)—have contributed to analysis of the 1944 Act, the paradigm shift of postsecular thought continues to encourage historical interpretation of the 1944 Act with an increased focus on its historic mandate of Religious Education. A postsecular approach not only helps unbury the Christian-civic humanism imbued in the 1944 Act but removes Butler's contributions from the dustbin of so-called Tory reactions to one of third-way and middle-opinion progressive legislation. British novelist Zadie Smith's *On Beauty* unwittingly helped me shift my liberal and secular historical lens to this view during my research: "Liberals never believe that conservatives are motivated by moral convictions as profoundly held as those . . . liberals profess . . . to hold. [They] . . . choose to believe that conservatives are motivated by a deep self-hatred, by some form of . . . psychological flaw. But . . . that's the most comforting fairy tale of them all!" (2005, 369).

After 9/11 and 7/7 a wider interest in postsecular historical analysis developed—a clear example is Callum Brown's *Religion and Society in Twentieth-Century Britain* (2006), offered in part as a revision to his *The Death of Christian Britain* (2001). In *Religion and Society* Brown revises his earlier claim for "the death of Christian Britain" rooted in the 1960s, and argues that since 9/11 "religion is back on the agenda" (xv). Although the scope of his work is much broader than a focus on Religious Education, he notes the anticipation of Christian social reformers and clergy such as Archbishop William Temple for gaining a foothold for Religious Education in England through the 1944 religious mandate. Again, Ofsted's 2007 report encouraged closer scrutiny of the history of Religious Education and collective worship arguing, "The notions, common until recently, that religion was quietly declining and Religious Education had little relevance to modern life now look naïve."

Examples of this work exist. Charmian Cannon's 1964 article, "The Influence of Religion on Educational Policy, 1902-1944," analyzes the cultural pressures surrounding Religious Education and its legislation as well as the religious convictions of the architects of the 1944 Act. Marjorie Reeves, ed., *Christian Thinking and Social Order: Conviction Politics from the 1930s to the Present Day* (1999) argues that important Christian intellectual voices of the 1930s must be carefully reconsidered because they were a key part of that historical record, regardless of the marginalization they have since suffered in intellectual, political, and educational history. Harris examines parts of this progressive intellectual thought—she mentions Butler, specifically—and its links to state welfare reform in the 1940s (1991, 1992, and 2003). Gregory Dochuk argues that Religious Education was linked to ideals for communal and corporate feelings in school and society (2006). Religious Education, Dochuk suggests, thus became a win-win policy for spreading religious culture, rather than a church-state political conspiracy. Matthew Grimley's work examines Christian intellectuals whose work was crucial to a Christian-civic humanist educational philosophy (2003 and 2007).

These are excellent studies to begin to understand why English politicians *mandated* (for the first time ever) Religious Education in 1944. Gaps in the scholarship, however, remain. To cite two examples: Brown's wide-ranging work notes a resurgence of British Christian culture in the 1940s and 1950s but does not offer a deeper discussion of how and why state-mandated Religious Education developed and was put into law. Furthermore, while Brown's claim for the "death of Christian Britain" in the 1960s is vital in English religious historiography, Religious Education and collective worship in schools remained mandatory post-1960—as Ofsted suggests, the time is ripe to continue investigations of how Religious Education influenced (and influences) students and English culture as a whole.

Logical historiographical reasons exist for the noticeable lack of attention to Religious Educational history and culture. Some scholarship focuses on the important dual control or church-state readings of the partnerships between the state and the church to maintain dual control in education (Cruickshank 1963). This work examines disputes and consensus among Christian denominations in terms of the content of Religious Education, yet these institutional and political analyses outnumber cultural analyses, with notable exceptions. In addition, mandatory Religious Education was not regarded as historically significant because it was interpreted as a short-lived reaction in the immediate postwar years and by the 1960s its specific Anglo-Christian characteristics were interpreted as beginning to give way to multiculturalism, interests in religious global politics, and increased secularism.

Interpretations of the 1944 Act have also tended to focus on the key concerns and debates over secondary education for all in English education. This emphasis was crucial in the 1944 Act's historical and historiographical context. Gary McCulloch and Liz Sobell, however, point out that the history of secondary education, like the history of Religious Education, is also incomplete (1994). They specifically suggest more work on the social history of secondary modern schools to explain why they emerged as part of the secondary educational reforms of the 1940s.

McCulloch and Sobell note that by the early 1960s almost 4,000 secondary moderns served over one and a half million children in England and Wales, but "the social and political significance of these schools, no less than their long-term historical importance, has still to be examined in any depth" (1994, 275). Fuller study of secondary modern schools reveals that secondary moderns were envisioned as a viable secondary school choice for the vast majority of students who would not attend university-prep grammar schools or specialized science and technology technical schools. This interpretation fits into my argument as well: Part of Butler's third-way thinking was in development of these types of institutions and that this work, married to the 1944 Act's mandate of Religious Education, was another piece of his third-way Christian-civic philosophy for educational reform. The calls for more research by Ofsted, McCulloch and Sobell, and others make clear the need for continued work on the history of education in England.

Again, this work has begun. In their extremely concise yet powerful analysis of the 1988 Educational Reform Act, with its necessary references to the legislation of the 1944 Act, Josephine M. Cairns and Edwin Cox note wasted chances in education following the legislation of the 1944 Act (1989). Cairns, for example, argues that post-1944, interpretations of the 1944 Act's educational proposals were constricted, in part by legislators who misjudged the realities of day-to-day school life. These limited views also contributed to historical interpretations of the 1944 Act which glossed over its Christian culture and state welfare ethics imbued within its rhetoric. With the benefit of twenty-first century historiographical shifts recharged focus on the making of the 1944 Act by Conservative and Christian thinkers and their collaborators is fruitful. This inquiry necessitates an introduction to Christian-civic humanism.

As a tradition, civic humanism is a difficult concept to pin down. As J. G. A. Pocock argues, early modern English republicans did not work from a republican paradigm, per se, but rather from accessible language and ideas (1975). Thus, Pocock's linguistic approach to political concepts is useful to analyze the flexible philosophies that Butler, Clark, and Mannheim promoted, which included not only republican and Christian ideals, but invoked third-way thinking that transcended partisan politics and generational divides. While Pocock applied his arguments of an "Atlantic republican tradition" to the upheaval of the English Revolution, his theoretical framework allows for broader interpretation and application, especially in regard to a broad definition of republicanism in interwar England: "civic humanism." This builds on a standard definition of civic humanism,

> [An] active, participatory, patriotic citizenship as well as the ethos and [the] educational ideal that goes with it . . . [It may include an] upsurge of patriotic [sentiment] as a response to foreign aggression and despotism, informed by the revival of classical [or traditional] models. This movement is also taken as a decisive turning point away from [old-fashioned] ways and towards liberating modernity. . . . Civic humanism is linked in principle to a[n] . . . educational program that goes beyond the formative capacity of participatory citizenship itself and involves the conscious revival of . . . [traditional] ideals. Republican candor, simplicity of manner, opposition to ostentation, luxury and lucre, are common . . . . Some theorists also dwell on the millenarian aspirations associated with republican ideals responding to the fragility of the republic and the need to provide against its corruption and decay with the passage of time (Stanford Encyclopedia of Philosophy 2008).

Pocock's analysis of this tradition suggests civic humanism as a concept was accessible to modern political reformers facing challenging, yet potential politically opportune, events in their national milieu.

The idioms of civic humanism fit Butler's and his colleagues' educational proposals. These were socio-political reactions to the threats against the British commonweal catalyzed by what Pocock might call the *occasione* of the interwar years: the political tyrannies, social and cultural decay, and ostentation brought on by modernist cultures and radical politics between the World Wars. Politicians and educationalists feared these events and reactions threatened the English nation's heart and soul: Anglo-Christian and civic traditions of liberty, justice, and truth.

Although in the twentieth century radical forms of English republicanism were often considered relics, republican language and ideals did not simply die out. They evolved and shifted with the times. By the twentieth century differences between democratic and republican systems were confused and confusing as the terms slipped and slid together in many political traditions: these concepts were not rigid agendas but fluid ideals. The British commonweal was based on classical ideals of Roman republicanism that balanced individual rights and civic responsibilities. The British Commonwealth, seen as a direct descendant of the Roman Empire, tried to balance its imperial rule with civic responsibility (Pocock 1975). The differences between republican and democratic ideals were sometimes just subtle emphases on the ultimate form of sovereignty: the rules of civic society or the equality of the citizens.

A use of civic humanist language or philosophy did not mean that Butler and his colleagues were attempting to create or re-create a viable political republic. It simply suggests that they were in tune with aspects of broadly-conceived republican ideals. Theirs was a wartime social reform project that sought to strengthen the existing political order through civic-mindedness rather than a political crusade to radically change the British government. Butler was not interested, for example, in overthrowing the monarchy, or dissolving parliamentary democracy for a direct democracy, but he was interested in strengthening and revitalizing the British political system through a synthesis of ideals taken from both democratic and republican traditions.

Butler, Clarke, and Mannheim's republican ideals were often couched in the language of democracy and socio-political enfranchisement. At the same time, Christian values and progressive ideas related to increasing civic and political participation within a democratic tradition were seen as integral to that socio-political tradition. Mannheim explained this choice succinctly: "As the emergence of Capitalism and the corresponding social revolutions occurred at a very early stage in England, when religion was still alive and permeated society as a whole, both the conservative and the progressive forces developed their philosophies within the set framework of religion" (1943, 110). Butler and Clarke were intimately familiar with republican, Christian, and commonweal ideals, traditions, programs, and language rooted in ancient Greco-Roman and Christian traditions as well as the radical republican tradition in English history. Both men alluded to them in their work with references to Plato, Milton, and other classical republican and Christian thinkers. Mannheim specialized in political sociology and democratic social planning and represented sociological expertise on these issues and proposals. An educational element was critical to this notion of Christian-civic humanism because Butler, Clarke, and Mannheim all believed that citizens must possess knowledge in order to function as responsible citizens.

At the same time their philosophy suggested an understanding that a republic can also refer to a system of restricted democracy. These restrictions included traditional forms of authority and cultural cohesion which for Butler and his colleagues included Christianity as a key form of moral and civilizing authority. In the English language these republican ideals were coded in the phrases commonweal, commonwealth or the British Commonwealth. Because, however, republic is often confusing given the events of the English Revolution, and commonwealth is complicated with the politics of the British Empire, the phrases Christian-civic humanism and commonweal, meaning "the public good," are used in this study to portray this ideology in opposition to the often misunderstood and slippery terms republicanism or commonwealth. The Christian-civic educational philosophy developed in the interwar era continued to be discussed and developed as the specters of Fascism and Communism threatened England physically and culturally in World War II. English politicians prepared themselves and the nation for an uncertain place in a new world order.

Domestic, as well as international issues, made Butler and his colleagues extremely anxious about the state of England. Trends of demographic decline suggested that British politicians must anticipate smaller future populations, making efficient planning of man [and woman] power a necessary and practical reality (Thane 1990). Thus anxieties about issues such as demographic decline in terms of Britain's economic and political role fundamentally shaped the 1944 Act. These trends and anxieties forced intellectuals and politicians to explore consensus-building and progressive reform that would not create further domestic havoc in the tumultuous years surrounding World War II. These trends suggested plans for state welfare using third-way politics.

A primary focus of Butler's plans for educational reform was the restoration of English socio-cultural and economic power through compromises among tradition, reform, and political reality. Mannheim described this kind of socio-political planning as "'Planning for Freedom' a Third Way between a laissez-faire society and total regimentation" (Mannheim 1951, xvii). Butler's movement reflects assessments of values of English third-way politics: "A belief in the value of community;" work as a "source of dignity and worth;" adherence to a "strong moral vein;" and the necessity of both individuals and public bodies to practice responsibility and accountability (Dickson 1999). Butler, Clarke, and Mannheim envisioned a "militant democracy" that insisted on a synthesis of traditional laissez-faire and modernist statist social and political policies. In addition, their brand of third-way ideology, Christian-civic humanism, encompassed a compromise between the growing divide between traditional and modernist cultural trends. This divide remained under the surface even during an era of consensus politics surrounding the Second World War. Mannheim argued, "The new militant democracy will . . . develop a new attitude to values. It will differ from the relativist laissez-faire of the previous age, as it will have the courage to agree on some basic values" (1943, 10). For Butler, Clarke, and Mannheim these basic values for England would be defined by the tenets of Christianity as a foundation of English culture. The "militant democracy" would mandate moral and spiritual education, encourage "planning for democracy," but hold an important distinction from statism: a "distinction between planning for uniformity and planning for freedom and variety" (Mannheim 1943, 10).

Community spirit would be developed through "political education" that encouraged active citizenship and social values that embraced all kinds of citizens (Butler 1939). Secondary and further education would be used to establish these social values and foster individuality by allowing student's aptitudes, interests, and abilities to guide them into intellectual, professional, industrial, agricultural, and service-industry fields necessary for the nation's commonweal. All forms of work that served the nation were valuable. As Dochuk reveals, Religious Education was meant to promote a strong moral vein, and communal worship would also help promote community solidarity (2006). Taken together, these elements would help promote state welfare.

The intellectual and structural components integral to the welfare of the state are apparent in the actual construction of the 1944 Act, including its moral and spiritual concerns, inclusive but varied educational tracks with a focus on youth services and further education, and its emphases on education as a lifelong, not just school-based, process. These elements formed the basis of the Christian-civic humanist educational philosophy. The relationship between Christian-civic humanism and ideas of commonweal, however, require an analysis of the differences between the Welfare State and a more broadly-conceived intellectual and political movement for state welfare.

An interesting question arises about what the Welfare State means as a concept versus other concepts of state welfare. Asa Briggs argues, "The phrase 'welfare state' is of recent origin. It was first used to describe Labour Britain after 1945" (1961, 2). Harris, however, suggests the intellectual and political thought that led to Brigg's interpretation of the Labour Welfare State—including the 1944 Act as a Welfare State policy—had a much longer reach in what she calls "social welfare history" and focuses in part on what she calls "the Welfare State policies of the 1940s" (1992, 233 and 1991, 135). The history of the Welfare State Harris examines suggests scrutiny of different readings of welfare state in addition to the interpretation provided by Briggs. Kathleen Woodroofe, for example, argues,

> The label 'Welfare State' is of recent origin. It was first used by Sir Alfred Zimmern during the 1930's [*sic*] to epitomize the contrast between warfare and welfare—the "guns or butter" of the Nazis—and later, by the Archbishop of Canterbury [William Temple] who, in 1941, published his *Citizen and Churchman* in which he developed the notion of a "welfare state" of the democracies as opposed to the "power state" of the dictators. The notion held, he argued, only if the state in the democracies fulfilled its moral and spiritual functions in promoting human welfare. The term was

> soon given a new connotation by the Beveridge Report in 1942 and the legislation of the Labour government which followed it, when the whole concept of welfare was widened from the pre-war concept of a set of social services for the care of people unable to care for themselves . . . (1968, 303-4).

Butler's ideas for education reform fit within the latter analyses of state welfare much more closely than an idea of a Labour Welfare State cradle to grave social system. Not coincidentally, both Zimmern and Temple were intimately connected with intellectual, political, and educationalist movements shaping Butler's 1944 Act.

In relation to the making of the 1944 Act, Butler, Clarke, and Mannheim developed proposals for state welfare issues, such as education during the interwar years, long before the passage of historic Labour Welfare State legislation. Another key, then, to understanding the 1944 Act's intellectual history is examining it as piece of interwar state welfare politics through third-way Christian-civic policies. After 1945, politicians, educationalists, and historians interpreted the 1944 Act differently as socio-political aims changed from promoting state welfare to promoting the Labour Welfare State. Whatever differences, however, exist between concepts of state welfare and the Welfare State, Butler did attempt to create compromises between the two in his plans for state-sanctioned Religious Education and "secondary education for all" in the 1944 Act. Nonetheless, his main goal was a state welfare educational policy within the rubric of Zimmern and Temple's understanding of state welfare as a democratic state fulfilling "its moral and spiritual functions in promoting human welfare," (Woodroofe 1968, 304) and practical theories of a guns *and* butter social welfare. Butler and his colleagues meant to serve the nation in "the battle of Education" and the "battle of the Young" (Butler 1942). For Butler, this was "a venture as important as [World War II] itself" (1942, 6). Thus, between 1941 and 1944, Butler's pledge: "having viewed the milk and honey from the top of Pisgah . . . I decided to disregard [Churchill's order and] go straight ahead [with education reform]." The result: the crystallization of Christian-civic educational thought codified in the 1944 Act.

Chapter 1 gives a general overview of the history of education in England through the early years of World War II. The chapter examines the historical context of English education in the nineteenth and early twentieth centuries to explain why and how secular and religious educational reforms were seen as necessary for social progress. Chapter 2 more deeply explores historiography surrounding the 1944 Act as mentioned in this introduction and includes reminders of noted scholars and works. Chapter 3 focuses on the history of educational philosophy in the interwar years, with special attention devoted to Butler, Clarke, and Mannheim as key members of an intellectual coalition that developed and synthesized the main tenets of the Christian-civic educational philosophy. Chapters 4 and 5 move into World War II when Butler became President of the Board of Education and transformed the intellectual ferment of interwar educational philosophies into underlying tenets of his 1944 Act. These chapters also explore political discussions surrounding the passage of the 1944 Act. Chapters 6 and 7 take a closer look at the two main pillars of Christian-civic humanism—Religious Education and secondary/further education—as embodied in educational discussions and the language of the 1944 Act. These chapters also examine their respective topics in terms of legislation and its interpretation, educational literature, and post-1944 legacies. This includes suggestions as to why historians, politicians, and the public often misinterpreted Butler and his colleagues' work in the postwar years.

CHAPTER ONE

A BACKDROP TO THE 1944 ACT

For in the night outside I see
Great storms preparing, from whose grips
I think shall come triumphantly
Only the noblest ships
—Quoted by R. A. Butler from Lord Dunsany, "Looking Seaward," 1935,
in conclusion to "The future of political education: an address," 1939

Two cornerstones of traditional English education are Religious Education and educational liberty. Although formal education was originally available to only select groups of students, typically from the upper classes, these tenets set important precedents for English pedagogy and curriculum. In the nineteenth century, the middle-classes argued for a popular expansion of education so that all citizens could be educated to better understand and engage in the responsibilities of civic and cultural life. Another interpretation of this era, however, argues that middle-class citizens believed that education was necessary for controlling and shaping the working classes. A fascinating theory, "the ideological roots of intelligence testing," argues that English educationalists equated abstract thinking and learning as crucial markers of the intellectual path to God and true spiritual illumination (White 2006). Both interpretations reveal the kind of Victorian values that shaped the expansion of formal English education in the nineteenth century.

Twentieth-century debates among educationalists also revolved around these issues. Some third-way thinkers looked for a synthesis between religious culture and secular politics as answers. In order to understand how and why these issues occupied their minds, the history of Religious Education, educational liberty, and their evolution into concepts of a specifically English definition of "secondary education for all" provide a historical backdrop. Because English national identity has been tied to a unique and public English-Protestant culture regardless of individual citizen's private beliefs and practices, Englishness remained tied to Christian ethics.

Indeed, historical and postsecular theories argue that contemporary society remains tied to traditional Protestant ethics. Religion was embedded in the fabric of English society through its traditional role in the service of education. Because the churches and educational services were traditional partners, Religious Education in English schools remained less controversial than in other countries. Religious Education disputes over denominational teaching in the nineteenth and twentieth centuries did, however, exist. These disputes were largely between and among Protestant sects over how to teach Christianity rather than between oppositional belief systems or demands for wholly secular state educational systems.

In England, shifts toward more representative governments had not created a secular state per se but rather a secular government with leaders who were still tied to the Church of England. The churches were responsible in large part for the formation of formal schooling in England—an education with obvious religious themes and curriculum. The state had made its first formal overture toward a national system of education in 1833 following the First Reform Act. The government offered a subsidy of 20,000 pounds toward building schools associated with the Nonconformist British and Foreign School Society and the Anglican National Society for Promoting the Education of the Poor. This subsidy tied the churches and the state together in a co-dependent relationship for providing education. Once established, this formal relationship bound the English government and the English churches into the dual system—church and state—of education that continues to this day.

By 1870 England passed the first of a series of Education Acts that strove to meet the nation's needs as a center of rising middle-class and professional power. The 1870 Education Act was done "[in] the typical English expedient of compromise by retaining the old system and grafting on it a new" (Cruickshank 1963, 37). The government planned to maintain efficiency and economy by allowing existing Anglican and Nonconformist schools to remain in place. The creation of the dual system in English education allowed the government simply to "fill up the gaps" left by religious bodies (Cruickshank 1963, 17). An expanded educational system served the needs of newly enfranchised middle-class populations and the state to keep British industry competitive in the second wave of industrialization. The government arranged to incorporate church schools into a national system by exchanging minimal government supervision (and responsibility) in return for state financial aid to help maintain infrastructure.

To settle religious difficulties which still divided Anglicans and Nonconformists, the state allowed schools that were voluntary, or run by a particular sect, to continue denominational education. Nevertheless, the 1870 Act's Cowper-Temple clause mandated that state-run schools be non-denominational. This did not mean state schools did not incorporate Religious Education. Rather, Cowper-Temple mandated no denominationally distinctive catechism or forms would be allowed in the curriculum or services. This was generally interpreted to refer to religious denominations within Christianity, although in some cases it extended to Judaism. Cowper-Temple was primarily designed, however, to dispel quarrels among English Protestant sects and assumed Religious Education had a place in the national educational system.

This legislation virtually ensured that Religious Education in some form would continue to be a part of English educational curriculums. Its removal would require major national reform that would offend powerful religious organizations. The Cowper-Temple clause also more or less guaranteed the permanence of the dual system because Anglicans, Nonconformists, and other religious or special-interest groups in England could only give specialized denominational instruction outside the confines of the state schools. Cowper-Temple, thus, led to disputes over what constituted non-denominational morals and ethics in England and a proliferation of voluntary schools and extra-curricular denominational Religious Education.

By 1900 the state organized a national Board of Education to provide a central educational authority. The Board's first major task was to put the 1902 Education Act into effect. The 1902 Act maintained both the dual system and the Cowper-Temple clause. Proposals were made to formally mandate Religious Education, but were dropped because the issue proved too controversial. There were thus few changes in provisions for Religious Education but the government integrated church schools more deeply into the national system by offering them financial assistance through rates. The state, however, took responsibility for the maintenance and salaries of teaching staff and for all secular education within state and voluntary schools. This move was in response to the failing efforts of voluntary schools to maintain educational infrastructure and to reform outdated curriculums.

In addition to the developments surrounding Religious Education in the 1902 Act, the state took also took a significant step in educational administration by disbanding school boards in favor of local educational authorities (LEAs). The local educational authorities had power over local elementary education and secular aspects of state-aided voluntary schools including some secondary and technical education. Educational liberty at the local level allowed each region to decide what kind of services to provide based on local populations and local concerns. Because local educational authorities had political and economic significance their liberty quickly became a factor in local political rights. Local authority remained an important tradition even as domestic and international trends for nationalized education began to evolve.

Political and educational officials realized, however, that the 1902 Act had not done enough to reform the system given educational and technological advances abroad. Educationalists argued for extending students' education by increasing the minimum age at which children could leave school. This transition was tied to proposals for the development of a broader secondary system to serve a more diverse student body, including more working-class children. Industrial and technological advances abroad, as well as the dispiriting Boer Wars, fueled fears that England was losing its industrial and military prowess. Voluntary schools continued to suffer from economic difficulties, which put the improvement of their curriculum into question and also suggested the necessity for increased state aid and control in the voluntary school sector.

The government believed educational reform, especially in terms of efficiency and economy within educational administration, was a key solution to these problems. Post-1902, the government maintained that national education was to remain "in the hands of experts instead of amateurs" (Cruickshank 1963, 86). Professional society, rather than the clergy, would handle England's educational future. The middle-classes had trained themselves for administrative duties during the nineteenth century: now they aimed to use these skills to educate the nation. The trick would be balancing central management with the local educational authorities. World War I, however, put educational evolution and reform on the back burner.

During the interwar years, however, it was clear to most politicians and intellectuals that domestic and international difficulties had not been settled by the World War I and that ideological as well as military conflicts would be reengaged. These issues developed into overarching debates about how to move forward: appeasement versus military engagement; a return to normalcy versus radical social and political reorganization; industrial capitalism versus nationalized socialism. Conservative-minded proposals perceived nihilism in some modernist and revolutionary politics and culture, but were not against a reform-minded and progressive society. By reviving traditional values such as patriotism, spirituality, and citizenship, proponents of middle opinion hoped to channel positive moral and spiritual energies into finding a path for England in the modern, industrialized world.

Within English education, interwar debates became focused on proposals for expanding secondary education. Although the government and leading politicians generally represented neo-liberal, moderate politics, a return to normalcy was difficult to achieve and progress appeared to be at a standstill. As attitudes hardened, the Left, especially socialist-leaning Labour circles, defined themselves as secular, modern, and radically progressive against a traditionalist, if not reactionary, brand of politics. Labour leader R. H. Tawney had introduced the key debate as early as 1922 when he coined the phrase "secondary education for all" as a proposal to provide primary and secondary education for all students regardless of class. This was a radical suggestion at the time because normally only upper and upper-middle class students, along with a few exceptional scholarship students from other classes, were given both. Although secondary education for all characterized a broad-spectrum of educational politics and proposals, its details split politicians and educationalists into broadly defined camps of egalitarians and those who favored plans to level the statuses of different types of education while maintaining diversity linked to laissez-faire ideals.

While politicians and educators generally agreed on the principle of secondary education for all their views differed in details and individual school programs. As Gary McCulloch (1994) has shown, the differences between the types of secondary education proposed were often finely shaded. A common goal of each was educational tracks that were diversified yet equivalent in status. The meaning of equality, however, was confused and contested within partisan debates. McCulloch has noted that one definition of equality was associated with the phrase "parity of esteem" as a desirable quality in education (1994). "Parity of esteem" could be interpreted as simply equal funding, services, and infrastructure for all secondary education. The national government had to decide if equality or parity of esteem were necessary or financially feasible.

In addition, interwar England was not yet fully committed to a national educational system funded solely by the state. Education was still reliant on private organizations and fees. The dual system of education by church and state remained an essential aspect of the system. Although the state increasingly gained authority over church-sponsored schools that required state funding, the national government was not economically prepared to provide church-affiliated and private schools with funding based on "parity of esteem" ideals. Maintaining the dual system allowed increased state control without nationalizing state spending on education. Thus, practical economics as well as tradition helped maintain a church-state relationship in education and figured into proposals for universal education.

Interwar politicians were also aware that increasing the school-leaving age or requiring universal secondary education for all meant financial hardship for the families of working-class students. Universal secondary education would also affect the labor supply as youth left work for school. C. P. Trevelyan, President of the Board of Education under Labour, proposed legislation between 1929 and 1931 for maintenance allowances to allow working-class children to leave work to attend secondary education without restricting their families' income. Although educationalists believed increasing the school-leaving age was a necessary step in English education, in the interwar years it was not a pragmatic economic—hence political—move. The Labour government failed to pass any of the three bills Trevelyan proposed. Trevelyan subsequently resigned from office stating his disgust with the Labour government's concern over the economy rather than social welfare.

This was an early and bitter fight in what would become a drawn-out battle between educational liberals and conservatives. Historical hindsight, however, suggests that the Labour party's educational plans and proposals for liberal secondary education for all were not rooted in egalitarian educational goals. Rather, Labour's education goals were tied to solving labor disputes and helping further develop liberally educated professional classes. Interwar educational reform and legislation were difficult to achieve because they were deeply complex social and economic issues. There were no simple answers. Contemporary debates over secondary education for all—as well as historically bitter debates over Religious Education—cast deep shadows over reform efforts. Although reformers continued to work toward consensus, their efforts were ultimately derailed by the social anxieties of the late interwar years.

England's interwar social anxieties over issues such as demographic decline were sometimes measurable, sometimes relative, and sometimes imagined. The mid-1930s saw a peak in forecasts giving dire predictions for an ageing British population. Social scientists such as Enid Charles published gloomy reports of demographic decline and concepts such as preventing social waste emerged in order to support commonweal. In this vein, education was seen as a tool to alleviate social waste by British politicians who took predictions of demographic decline seriously and planned accordingly for increasing economic and labor efficiency. The need to maintain and produce citizens who could work within the various sectors of the socio-economic system focused attention on educational reform as an avenue to bolster the perceived shrinking pool of workers and services. Fears of demographic decline linked to fears of continued economic stagnation contributed directly to ideas about secondary education for all that would help support a diverse workforce. Social scientists and educational psychologists such as Cyril Burt promoted use of psychological and intelligence testing in educational planning to protect Britain against "the menace of underpopulation" (Charles 1936).

In the wake of Trevelyan's failures to pass a more radical system of secondary education for all educationalists and politicians compromised to pass the 1936 Education Act. This Act put in place progressive policies in education to help soothe interwar anxieties. The Act proposed free, although not compulsory, education up to age fifteen along the lines of earlier reform proposals for expanded secondary education and training. The Act also laid groundwork for further development of Religious Education to counter social and cultural pressures of the interwar years. Although it set precedents, the Act's effectiveness was hampered. Domestic controversies and disturbing international events delayed the Act's implementation, eventually making its key legislation moot. Denominational controversies, notably, marred its smooth passage into accepted practice.

Nevertheless, in the aftermath of the 1936 Act, Christian intellectuals working largely outside of official educational and political arenas attempted to promote progressive Religious Education and ecumenical Christian spirit. The 1937 Oxford Conference, a gathering of Christian leaders from around the globe, met in response to disturbing global trends and events. Focusing especially on those issues they associated with "challenges to Christian thought" conference delegates paid close attention to issues that "caught" Christians "between nationalism on one side and communism on the other" (Aubrey 1937, 380). These concerns narrowed in on those groups seen as particularly vulnerable: students and youth. A conference report outlined the challenges Christian leaders believed were faced by the world at large and suggested that increased Religious Education could help guide youth in the troubled interwar years. Key concerns were that struggles against economic depression had fueled the popularity of Fascist and Communist solutions (Aubrey 1937). Conference delegates also analyzed internal challenges faced by Christians with a particular reference to the lack of preparation Christian leaders had made toward issues including gender, race, and denominational conflicts (Aubrey 1937). The final address given at the Oxford Conference focused specifically on reformed Religious Education in England and other "so-called Christian nations" with educational proposals based on four main tenets: Theology should be made "relevant to current life;" Religious Education should be based upon a "philosophy and psychology of education;" Religious Education should provide "a program . . . for youth in a rapidly moving world;" and as an entity, it should "mould public opinion governing educational policies" (Aubrey 1937, 393). Clearly, Christian educationalists believed religious life could act as an anchor for the generations developing in the midst of global angst and flux.

Although educationalists raised a host of issues related to a reformed structure, by the late 1930s educational provisions for universal secondary education (and thus extended Religious Education) had not been achieved. A key political question remained: How to provide secondary education for all without unnecessary social conflict? The debate centered on what were seen as divergent issues of human justice and national economy. Members of the Board of Education's Consultative Committee argued in their 1938 Spens Report that human justice was best served by allowing individuals to seek education best suited to their aptitudes and interests. Not only did this fit into a liberal tradition, but it allowed the creation of a more diverse workforce to serve a democratic and industrialized economy. The Spens Report suggested multilateral schools could be united by the common goals of a basic liberal curriculum—including Religious Education.

Nevertheless, more radical educationalists, such as members of the National Association of Labour Teachers (NALT), believed that human justice could only be achieved if all children were educated under the same roof. The Labour Teachers argued, "Instead of providing different types of school for the over-elevens, the State should provide a single type for all children. . . . There is a distinct social stratification in the system of post-primary education" (NALT 1939, 6-7). Students who did not receive this type of comprehensive education represented wasted potential and social stratification harming the national spirit. These two camps appeared to be diametrically opposed about the direction education should take.

Conventional wisdom regarding the interwar years focused almost single-mindedly on these divisive issues. Nonetheless, although educationalists differed on the structure[s] a reformed system should take, social and intellectual consensus on long-term goals, if not actual legislation, did exist. In the increasingly difficult years following the 1936 Act, social angst in England increased as the country was drawn into another war. Educationalists took interwar policy proposals and began to develop them for additional educational reform proposals and consensus measures. These measures often directly related to combating the shadow of totalitarianism engulfing Europe.

These issues came to a climax with England's entry into World War II. Major concerns included the effect of the war on young people and concern that ideals of Fascist youth programs "in the totalitarian countries" might infect youth programs in England (Holmes 1939; Gosden 1976, 210). In response, a 1939 government circular, "The Service of Youth" worked to attend to English youth and bring their welfare under more stringent state influence. The circular set precedent that the Board of Education would take accountability for youth welfare including continuing social and physical training for school leavers up to the age of twenty. Although further plans for youth services were laid out, popular perceptions of overt militarism and latent fascism within the circular had a chilling effect on these proposals as Fascist youth programs abroad became abhorred.

Yet by 1940 war-time chaos and destruction such as the bombing of London led to a creeping general malaise, including reports of increased juvenile delinquency. Some youth groups had found success in providing services to young people, especially outside the London area and within voluntary organizations (Gresh 1940). Nevertheless, the perceived need for increased moral training and educational reform deepened following popular and practical observation of London war-time evacuees. *The Times* reported in two 1940 articles, "Slum Life in Cities" and "Religion and the National Life," that middle- and upper-class rural families who took in London evacuees were shocked at their lack of decorum and became alarmed that "problem families" within the heart of England faced a future with a "purely heathen upbringing." "Slum Life" argued many rural families found children from London they received in their homes to be "destructive and defiant, foul-mouthed, liars and pilferers." "Religion and the National Life" deepened anxieties by reporting that many "town children" had no religious knowledge at all, knew nothing of the Bible, and "had never been taught to pray." "Slum Life" further stirred the pot of brooding fears regarding demographic decline and upswings in juvenile delinquency for the so-called "submerged tenth."[3]

[3] William Booth coined the term "submerged tenth" in his *In Darkest England and the Way Out* (1890) to represent the bottom socio-economic tenth of the English population following Charles Booth's investigations into English slums in the late nineteenth century. *The Times* borrowed this phrase for their reporting in "Slum Life in Cities" (1940). The evacuation of schoolchildren during World War II revealed, once again, the social, cultural, and educational lags in England's working class populations.

The Times argued, “the ‘submerged tenth,’ described by Charles Booth, still exists in our towns like a hidden sore—poor, dirty, and crude in its habits, an intolerable and degrading burden to decent people forced by poverty to neighbor with it.” These reports catalyzed reform efforts within the educational system to provide better training for teachers and students. Specific calls were also made for Religious Education within the state educational system. “Religion and National Life” argued “The truth, of course, is that religion must form the very basis of any education worth the name, and that education with religion omitted is not really education at all.” This was a starting point in World War II popular media requests for legislation of Religious Education as the solution for domestic decline. Soon Religious Education would also be proffered as a potent weapon against Fascist ideologies.

On February 12, 1941, the Archbishops of Canterbury, York, and Wales released an official statement on “True Christian Education” reprinted in *The Times*. The Archbishops argued, “There is an ever deepening conviction that in this present struggle we are fighting to preserve those elements in human civilization and in our own national tradition which owe their origin to Christian faith.” The Archbishops’ “appeal for ‘True Christian Education’” and “effective training for citizenship” argued that “in all schools a Christian education [be provided and] . . . entrusted to teachers willing and competent to give it.” The “Five Points,” as the statement came to be known, made clear the relationship between Christian and civic virtues in English society. These issues would continue to be addressed by educationalists and politicians in the days and weeks that followed.

The General Secretary of the National Union of Teachers (NUT), for example, sent a letter to Board of Education official Maurice Holmes on February 27, 1941 presenting his support for a national syllabus of Religious Education to counter “the new humanism underlying present school methods,” and to unify and improve Religious Education curriculums across the country. On May 5, Holmes received another letter, this time from The Rev. Canon Spencer Leeson, headmaster, The College, Winchester and Bishop of Peterborough. Leeson was working in collaboration with the Conservative MP Lord Wolmer and other educationalists and Christian leaders in forming a “Council of the Religious Education Movement” which was seeking agreements, as a precursor to legislative proposals, on matters of an agreed religious syllabus for schools and a statement of “central belief.” Holmes’ response indicated that he and others at the Board had been working on issues of reforming the church-state dual system and were open to Leeson's and

Wolmer's work and suggestions. Holmes stated, however, that he would refrain from approaching the President of the Board of Education Herwald Ramsbotham until Ramsbotham could confirm the priorities and wishes of the LEAs and teachers. Ramsbotham's influence, however, was to be short-lived. His position was soon jeopardized by discussion of potentially controversial educational issues as well as political and diplomatic ineptitude. Legislation would have to wait, yet consensus on educational reform initiatives had already begun—outside the confines of the Board of Education—by Ramsbotham's replacement, R. A. Butler.

Butler's work as chair of the Conservative Party Central Education Committee had put him into contact with like-minded educationalists. Butler had also made public statements about his views on education which put in him compatible company: his 1938 *A National Faith: By a Modern Conservative* was published by Geoffrey Faber. Faber's publishing house, Faber & Faber, released a number of works on Christianity and education during the interwar and early war years, including works by J. H. Oldham. Faber, in return, served as a collaborator on the *Christian News-Letter*, edited by Oldham between 1939 and 1945. The *News-Letter* focused on Christian concerns, including heavy focus on links between politics, education, and religion. Key collaborators in this intellectual and public mission also included Fred Clarke, Karl Mannheim, the Archbishop of York, William Temple, and a variety of other 1930s and 1940s intellectuals and educationalists. Not surprisingly, *News-Letter* collaborators overlapped with the membership of another Oldham organization—the Moot.

By June 1941 Butler served as chair of the Conservative Postwar Problems Committee. He used this position to begin formation of sub-committees including a Conservative Sub-committee on Education with Faber as chair. Butler wrote to Faber in a letter dated June 26, 1941, "I am keen to secure people to run these Committees who are of the Conservative faith but are yet outside the party machine." The committees that Butler organized came to include a variety of men and women from diverse political and educationalist backgrounds including members of Parliament, academics, and educationalists. Many had previously met in Christian intellectual organizations to address issues and problems in education during the war and to plan for the postwar years. These groups brought together overlapping circles of leading educationalists, including Butler, into an intellectual milieu of Christian-civic thinkers (see figure 1-1) committed to educational reform as their contribution to solving existing interwar and emerging World War II problems.

Moot (c. 1938)
J. H. Oldham, founder
Members included:
Fred Clarke,
T. S. Eliot,
P. Mairet,
Walter Moberly,
Archbishop William Temple,
(correspondent)

Christian News-Letter (c. 1939)
J. H. Oldham, editor
Collaborators included:
Fred Clarke,
Geoffrey Faber,
Karl Mannheim,
T. S. Eliot,
R. H. Tawney,
Walter Moberly,
Archbishop William Temple,
Walter Oakeshott,
Sir Walter Moberly,
Sir Alfred Zimmern

All Souls Group (c. 1941)
W. G. S. Adams, founder
Members included:
Fred Clarke,
H. C. Dent,
John Newsom,
R. A. Butler (guest member)

Conservative Committee on Post-war Problems (c. 1941)
R. A. Butler, chair
Sub-committee members included:
Geoffrey Faber,
T. S. Eliot,
Karl Mannheim,
Walter Oakeshott,
Fred Clarke (correspondent)

Faber & Faber (1938–1949)
(Selected publications)
R. A. Butler, 1938, "Preface," *A National Faith*
J. H. Oldham, 1941, *The Church Looks Ahead*
T. S. Eliot, 1941, *Towards a Christian Britain*
R. A. Butler, 1943, "Preface," *Forward from Victory*
R. A. Butler, 1948, "Preface," *The Education of Girls*
Gordon Ette, 1949, *For Youth Only*

Fig. 1-1: These groups brought together overlapping circles of leading educationalists into an intellectual milieu of Christian-civic thinkers committed to educational reform as their contribution to solving existing interwar and emerging World War II issues and problems.

In the twentieth century, the preservation of Religious Education in schools became an issue with international as well as domestic implications: Religious Education was seen as a key cultural and educational difference between England and totalitarian regimes. This ideology was noted by politicians such as the President of the Board of Education, R. A. Butler, in a number of statements in Parliament and on educational reform including a 1942 speech to the NUT and in the "The

Future of Political Education" in the House of Lords, (1944). Many English officials and intellectuals suggested English Religious Education was an essential difference between English national character and Fascist trends.

Although Butler and his like-minded colleagues had begun to lay the foundations for this educational reform in the late interwar years, their movement required time, patience, and money. All three became increasingly scarce when England entered World War II virtually alone against the Nazi threat. Yet, as the interwar era came to a close with the reality of a new war, the work of intellectuals and educationalists in England became more pressing. Educational reform movements had taken small steps forward in the interwar years but would face roadblocks put in place by the military crises of World War II.

Prime Minister Winston Churchill had long predicted the Nazi threat to England. Before England entered the war Churchill had already spent years trying to convince the English government to stiffen their foreign policy in the face of German rearmament. Appointed a member of the War Cabinet in 1939, Churchill was more than ready when he became Prime Minister to focus on the war effort in terms of military and international issues. Because Churchill's focus in the early years of the war was strictly on the war effort, any initiative for social change and postwar reconstruction fell on the shoulders of subordinates, especially in terms of the Conservative party where leadership was less favorable to reform to begin with. Given England's fragile position in the early years of World War II, Churchill's concerns remained focused on the war effort rather than domestic reforms. Government officials were pressured to avoid domestic problems and the potential controversies they could engender.

Indeed, the early war years resulted in little postwar planning at the official government level. Churchill's Minister of Economic Warfare, Hugh Dalton, famously noted in his memoirs, "[Churchill was] allergic to postwar policy," especially actions that might threaten his leadership or the coalition (410). In fact, several reports suggest that in June 1941 Churchill removed President of the Board of Education Ramsbotham from office because his education policy statement, the 1941 Green Book, "Education after the War," was seen to be stirring up trouble.

Ramsbotham's proposals, although they had been publicized before their publication, had been kept to a narrow group of individuals (Barber 1994). Other interested officials, for example, Parliamentary Secretary for Education James Chuter Ede, had to instruct his private secretary to make an official request to receive a copy (Chuter Ede 1987). This gave Ramsbotham's proposals an air of secrecy and mystique that rattled those who took an interest in matters of education. Ironically, the Green Book was relatively mild, containing proposals stemming from Consultative Committee reports including the 1938 Spens Report. These proposals reflected educational proposals that had been hashed out since at least 1922. Their publication and passage, however, required a softer touch.

Butler, an experienced and diplomatic politician, had been working on issues of progressive reform for at least five years and had already met with and synthesized the advice of intellectuals and educationalists. This groundwork proved crucial because Butler's entry at the Board of Education and his plans for educational reform were fraught with challenges from his very appointment. In fact, it is suggested, although the historical records differ on this matter, that Churchill's choice to put Butler at the Board of Education in 1941 was planned as an insult to Butler's political career. This was seen as Churchill's retaliation for earlier conflicts with Butler over India and appeasement (Butler 1971). Others argue that Churchill had little respect for education and he saw the Board position as a convenient place to stick Butler, out of the way as it were, during the war (Howard 1987). Butler, however, did not shy away from this appointment. In fact, he eagerly accepted his tenure at the Board of Education (Butler 1971) and chose to stay at the Board of Education throughout the war, despite evidence that indicates he was put on a short-list for his dream job as Viceroy of India (Howard 1987). Butler entered office as the President of the Board of Education on July 20, 1941 with an education philosophy in hand and a plan of action in mind.

Less than two months after he took office, on September 12, 1941, Butler sent Prime Minister Churchill a letter outlining what he had found in his first weeks as President of the Board of Education to be "the questions immediately before the Board." He proceeded to describe projects on which he would focus his attention for the next few years: industrial and technical training for "the linking up of schools closely with employment." Butler told Churchill that "the machinery of education becomes increasingly ill-adapted to present-day requirements" and that, "The apprentice system is in decline, and something is needed in its place if we are to keep in the forefront of industrial production." Instead of a Communist or Socialist-style comprehensive system, however, he believed the minds and lives of workers could be improved through, "more expert training for Industry . . . a revivified system of apprenticeship and a practical form of continued education [for workers and others]." Thus, national and individual benefits could be ensured through a re-vitalization of these aspects of education and working-class culture. This working-class culture would not be limited to a reified socio-economic system but would encompass a broader effort to train men and women to serve their individual and national interests according to personal interest, aptitude, and ability. The crux of Butler's letter proposed educational reform that did not "rush into legislation" but which immediately began to address these significant issues in English education in order to "harness the spirit of the times to the cause of social reform . . . to save ourselves and our civilization . . . [and] build for the future." This would be Butler's contribution to the war effort.

Butler also made clear he would not avoid addressing potentially controversial issues during the war including the dual system and Religious Education. These issues increased the difficulty of his task. In his memoir, Butler recalls Churchill's explicit instructions to avoid initiating educational reform during the tumultuous war years with specific regard to religious instruction.

> [Churchill argued,] it would be the greatest mistake to raise the 1902 controversy during the war, and I certainly cannot contemplate a new Education Bill. . . . No one can possibly tell what the financial and economic state of the country will be when the war is over. . . . We can not have any party politics in wartime and . . . your points [on educational reform] raise these in a most acute and dangerous form (1971, 94).

Regardless of Religious Education's historical controversy, however, the Board of Education and Prime Minister Churchill's office were receiving letters and requests to consider Religious Education reform from concerned citizens and officials—some intimate enough with the Prime Minister to address his wife by personal endearments. In addition, Lord Wolmer led seventy-two members of Lords and 151 members of Commons to submit a signed request for Religious Education to the Prime Minister's office. The "Christian Education" memo demanded that the "elemental principles of the Christian philosophy of life," "Truth, Freedom and Justice," be rekindled across the nation through Religious Education. Wolmer noted in his September 15, 1941 letter that these members of Parliament, "include[ed] members of all political parties, and . . . free Churchmen and Anglicans."

This Parliamentary romance with Christian ethics suggested a plan to make "the future citizen . . . so moulded in character by Christian education that his citizenship shall become the expression of these principles in action" (Wolmer 1941). In response to Lord Wolmer on the subject of Religious Education, Churchill refused to comment, although he assured Wolmer that the issue was being carefully considered. Wolmer's argument that, "wherever I go I find there is tremendous feeling among all sorts of people . . . that this opportunity must be taken to put Christian Education on a surer foundation" gave Butler firmer standing on the broader issue of educational reform. By September 18 Butler informed Churchill by letter, as diplomatically as possible, that he would continue working on issues of educational reform. A fascinating hand-written note signed "WC September 21" on this letter reads: "But we shall have to fight hard not to be conquered meanwhile [in which case] the Hitler Youth Organization [would] be the model."

Butler's passionate work in- and outside the Board of Education fueled these developments. His nascent Christian-civic political philosophies were honed by like-minded Christian-civic thinkers. The work of two men, Fred Clarke and Karl Mannheim, represents clear educational and sociological influences. Beyond the communication between politicians and administrators on these issues, Butler, Clarke, and Mannheim were clearly connected by intellectual and collaborative threads in these interwar and World War II years. Clarke and Mannheim, notably, were vital connections between these Christian groups and the world of formal education at the Institute of Education. Indeed, Clarke's biographer, Frank Mitchell argues that Mannheim and Clarke were working so closely as colleagues that attempting to separate their ideas and influence on each other was difficult, if not impossible (1967). By 1940 Butler and Mannheim had also met with common purpose and Butler and Clarke were traveling in the same circles. The continental European Mannheim's association with English intellectuals was a particularly opportune meeting of minds in the turbulent interwar years. His contributions helped solidify educational reconstruction efforts by introducing an academic sociological legitimacy to the ferment of social reform in the late interwar years.

CHAPTER TWO

THE 1944 ACT AS HISTORY

> [The] heroic, populist, and utopian constructions of national identity and citizenship [that] dominated public and political culture during the war years . . . did not have singular meanings, they differed.
> —Sonya O. Rose, *Which People's War?*

R. A. Butler's 1944 Education Act's educational philosophy developed during the interwar years, coalesced during World War II, and was embedded into law and revealed to the public in the mid-1940s. Despite the subsequent failures and criticism of the 1944 Act, Butler and his educationalist colleagues' motivations for Christian-civic humanism for state welfare were as profound as the convictions of champions of Welfare State schemes. Yet the newly-elected Labour government's focus on Welfare State projects in the postwar years overshadowed Butler's Christian-civic humanist educational plans. As a result, in the decades that followed, secondary education in England became characterized more and more as an issue left unsolved by the 1944 Act. Indeed, the "great debate," as it was framed by Prime Minister James Callaghan in 1976, continues to be a driving force—for better or worse—in English education.

Some historians, Stephen Fielding argues, added to the partisan nature of these issues through biased political interpretations:

> Many of those who wrote in the labour history tradition shared the political assumptions of the 'movement's' activists. When these beliefs failed to explain events, both activist and historian retreated behind accustomed thinking, hoping the world would go away (1995, 48).

Educational history written under the influence of the labor history tradition includes analysis of the 1944 Act. Critical examination of this historiography helps shed new light on 1930s and 1940s educationalists' convictions, as does work by Gary McCullough and Jose Harris, who consider the 1944 Act as an intellectual and educationalist plan to influence civil society through education. McCullough and Harris leave room in the discussion, however, to further consider Christian tenets of the 1944 Act and how they were meant to work in sync with civic humanism.

Contemporary historiographical trends including the "crisis in labour history," as well as examination of Western identity politics related to Islamophobia, have encouraged reexamination of religious culture using postsecular methodologies. By examining the 1944 Act's legislation for Religious Education alongside practical proposals for secondary and further education—a goal of this study—scholars begin to expose the educational philosophy of Christian-civic humanism vital to fleshing out the historical record. These research trends have also generated a resurgence of interest in middle-opinion political theories and ideals related to Christian thought. These issues all suggest an on-going need for historical reassessment of the 1944 Act.

Three historians greatly influenced this work: Marxist historian of education, Brian Simon; intellectual historian, Jose Harris; and historian of religion, Callum Brown. Simon, a contemporary of the 1944 Act, as well as its most famous historian and critic, deserves close analysis for his significant work in the history of education and his role as an activist within educational politics. Harris' more recent revisionist intellectual histories recognize Butler and his colleagues as state welfare intellectuals and are crucial to historians attempting to understand the intellectual background for the civil society Butler and his cohort wished to create. Brown's noted work in *The Death of Christian Britain: Understanding Secularization, 1800-2000* (2001) and *Religion and Society in Twentieth-Century Britain* (2006) on religion and secularization theories provide important background for British twentieth century religious and secularization history but, as Brown himself states, following 9/11 these issues demand new scrutiny.

The late Brian Simon was a widely influential historian, professor of education, and educational activist for nationalized, comprehensive schooling in England. Geoff Whitty, director of the University of London, Institute of Education, called Simon "arguably the most famous education historian of all time" who "will continue to inspire generations of teachers and students" (2003). Simon's histories of education clearly symbolized shifts in traditional nineteenth and early twentieth century educational historiography toward post-World War II Marxist interpretations. As William Richardson argues: "Simon directly espoused this method" and made "class conflict . . . the principal focus of historical study among educationalists" (Richardson 1999, 15-16). Thus, analyses of Simon's scholarly work are fundamental to deconstructing key debates of twentieth-century English educational and social history.

Simon's activist and professional reach in education, however, was also widely influential. Therefore, his personal and political work as an educationalist and activist require consideration in tandem with analysis of his historiography. As a noted critic of the 1944 Act, Simon's contributions to the educational historiography of Butler and his colleagues' philosophy may benefit from such consideration. While Simon's works in the history of education remain foundational studies his death in 2002 has allowed deeper critical analysis of his role as a primary source to begin alongside historiographical analysis of his histories. Simon's first major educational history, *Studies in the History of Education, 1780-1870* (1960), is regarded as having made "a significant reorientation [in the history of education] by an educationalist from hagiography to radical critique" (1999, 15). This review was meant as high praise in an era when educational systems were under critical scrutiny. Citations of his work, however, often ignore Simon's activist role in making some of the very history he wrote about as a historian.

Simon was a long-term British educationalist as well as a long-time member of the Communist Party. As a result, Simon's historical analyses became linked to committed Marxist principles. Simon joined the British Communist Party in 1935 and served in the party executive from 1956 to 1972. As Richard Aldrich notes in *Education and Policy*, Simon's commitment to Communism was "no mere youthful indulgence" (1991, 73). As noted, one of his greatest triumphs as a Marxist scholar and activist was rooting the history of education in England as a struggle between classes. This included, most notably, his interpretations of the making, implementation, and legacy of the 1944 Act in *Education and the Social Order* (1991).

Yet Simon's activism connected him to making this history, not just writing about it. This included a personal and professional crusade to reform the flaws (as Simon saw them) of the 1944 Act, exemplified by his leadership role in the Comprehensive Schools Committee (CSC). Simon described the CSC in *Education and the Social Order* as "a well organized pressure group of comprehensive supporters . . . formed to monitor developments and to press for radical change" (281). He ultimately characterized the 1944 Act as a failure and a betrayal having "left things fundamentally as they were [before 1944] . . . [a system that] serve[d] the needs of a class-divided society . . . not able to utilize the abilities of all its citizens, and so dare not develop them to the full" (1953; 1971, 45 and 48).

Simon did not try to veil, per se, his political and personal activities and influences. In fact, he argues in the introduction of *Education and the Social Order*, "I have not tried to hide my own position and my own interpretation of these developments," nor, "my own direct involvement in education" (1991, 16-18). He could, perhaps, have been more transparent about these issues in the text. In regard to the CSC, for example, he mentions his involvement with the formation of the group in a footnote, and there refers to himself in the third person (1991, 333). He does not acknowledge his Communist affiliations in the book, although he does examine controversies and problems surrounding Communist-affiliated educationalists such as the "Middlesex Ban" against Communist and Fascist teachers begun in 1950. Simon argues, "The singling out of Communists as a threat . . . acted to downgrade education issues with which they were particularly concerned and committed. Chief among these was the comprehensive school [campaign]" (1991, 121-5; 146).

Simon's personal and familial connections and his socio-political philosophies are also cloudy in the text. Simon's immediate and extended family, including his wife, Joan [Peel] Simon, an educationalist, social reformer, and historian in her own right, were directly involved in educational and social reform movements from the interwar years to the end of the century. The extended Simon family served in a variety of venues in educational reform, including taking academic, social, and political stands against psychometric testing, and was in favor of radical educational reforms such as comprehensive schooling. Yet in the 1991 text, Simon's relationship to his parents, Sir Ernest and Lady Shena Simon, is less than rigorously transparent, given their relationship to Simon, and their personal background and standing in social and educational circles.

In his introduction to *Education and the Social Order* Simon thanks "both my parents, who individually played their own different parts in this saga and with whom, of course, many of the issues here dealt with were discussed, frequently and at length" (1991, 20). He does not here, however, mention Sir Ernest or Lady Shena Simon by name. He does not specifically mention his mother's intricate involvement with further education, despite her prominent involvement in education before, during, and after the 1944 Act. In fact, in *Education and the Social Order*, Simon does not acknowledge by formal identification that Lady Simon was his mother at all, although he refers to her in the book six times by name and quotes her as a "percipient and closely involved observer" (1991, 17). He mentions his father Sir Ernest Simon of Wythenshawe six times as well but again without formally acknowledging their relationship. He refers to his wife Joan [Peel] Simon eleven times and acknowledges her in his dedication and introduction. He also notes her position at the *Times Educational Supplement* during the making of the 1944 Act, as well as his relationship to her at this time. Simon's parents and wife were involved in educational and other social and political issues by their own initiative. While debatable how transparent a historian need be about the personal context of his or her work, these relationships reveal much about Simon's personal involvement in educational reform.

What Simon's interpretation of the 1944 Act and its legacy reveals, then, is not just a history of education but also a critical analysis of that history based in part on personal involvement in making that history. Interrogating Simon's work thus reveals his position in the developing postwar generation gap, although Simon's admiration for older educationalists like Fred Clarke is noted. In 1940, at age 60, Clarke spoke positively of the possibilities for educational and social changes in England. Simon's analyses of education and society, begun in the 1940s—while in his twenties—would counter that view with arguments about stagnation and continued class conflict in English "education and the social order." This generation gap in ideology also firmly separated Simon from Butler. This is clarified in part by their individual approaches to educational reform and politics.

In 1943, as a 28-year-old student at Cambridge, Simon wrote "A Student's View of the Universities," a radical critique of the university system. This publication was symbolic of his career as a radical educationalist and activist. By the passage of the 1944 Act, Butler was 42. By 1944, Butler had established himself as a progressive Conservative politician and leader working on one of the defining state welfare projects of his political career. Simon was still in the early stages of his career as a radical educator, social activist, and historian of education. Simon's work focused on critiquing education policy and philosophy partly in response to left-wing goals for a Welfare State. Ironically, Butler and Simon had similar goals—social and educational reform—but they had very different ideas about how this reform should be accomplished. In Butler's mind, the 1944 Act was a New Conservative initiative that sought to smooth over fault lines in culture and society by stabilizing traditional social bedrock in order to aid the renovation of existing structures. Simon saw the Act as a betrayal of a Labourite Welfare State and its presumed path toward socialism by Conservative conspirators.

Simon regarded the 1944 Act as a potentially revolutionary piece of Welfare State legislation, in line with Labour reforms as a first step toward socialism. In the course of his study he tends to tie delays and problems in education under Labour after 1945 to decisions made by "Tory" politicians. Butler serves as a key scapegoat. For example, Simon argues that problems in education and educational finance were linked to "crucial decisions made *before* Labour's victory of July 1945" (1991, 103). He also blames post-1945 difficulties on Butler's economic policies as Chancellor of the Exchequer and the "cheeseparing" initiatives they forced on the Labour Board of Education (1991, 162-3). A broader analysis, however, reveals Labour as maintaining postwar austerity and promoting conservative educational policies during its 1945-1951 reign. Scrutiny of Simon's historical analysis with the benefit of twenty-first century hindsight reveals that aspects of Simon's scholarship contain historiographical biases.

In *Education and the Social Order*, for example, Simon discusses interwar reformist movements in education in line with his Marxist educational philosophies. His sympathies lay with what he calls "[radically] progressive," "radical," (i.e. largely multilateral structures he believed would develop into comprehensive schools) and "democratic programme[s]" of Labour party officials such as R. H. Tawney (1991, "The Second World War and Education"). Simon represents Tawney, the interwar educationalist who coined the phrase "secondary education for all," as the founding father of a comprehensive movement that favored radical egalitarianism in education akin to Simon's own postwar personal crusades for comprehensive schooling and the abolition of intelligence testing. Investigation of Tawney's record and background, however, suggests alternative interpretations of his interest in "secondary education for all." Tawney's *Secondary Education for All* (1922) indicates that Tawney's main goal was not egalitarian comprehensives, but simply universal free secondary education for all in contrast to a divided system of elementary and secondary education.

Tawney's radicalism in education is further brought into question by Sheila C. Blackburn's 1999 analysis that regards him "to be more concerned with moderate (and in his opinion, workable) policies rather than radical ideas" (107). These readings suggest Tawney was interested in secondary education for all along lines similar to Butler's and Clarke's brand of Christian-civic humanism for state welfare. Although this interpretation is subject to historical debate, Simon's work fails to mention strong connections between Tawney and key 1940s Christian intellectuals and educationalists. Tawney's relationship with Clarke, for example, raises questions about Simon's analysis of Tawney's call for secondary education for all.

Interestingly, although Simon does not discuss connections between Tawney and Clarke, Simon does express admiration for Clarke's work in passing. He notes, for example, Clarke's fresh approach and his introduction of a "sociological dimension" to English educational discussions (1991, 40). He also notes the influence Karl Mannheim had on educational philosophies. Despite this praise, Simon's treatment of policy groups related to Clarke's influence—notably, the Conservative Sub-committee on Education—in *Education and the Social Order* is glancing. In the book Simon provides a sketchy analysis of the Sub-committee at best (1991, 65-6 and 84). This treatment seems peculiar given the decades-long research Simon and his wife began in the 1940s focused in part on the 1944 Act and during the years the Sub-committee was in session. Indeed, Simon argues in *A Life in Education*, "I was never out of touch with wartime educational developments" (1998, 45). Simon's *Education and the Social Order* footnotes, rather than the body of his argument, give the fullest discussion of the Conservative Sub-committee reports. Given the importance of the Committee's work, this decision seems curious, but careful reading shows that his analysis of the Conservative Sub-committee appears to rely on his reading of secondary sources—notably Dennis Dean's and Jose Harris' work—although he lists the Sub-committee's reports in his bibliography. Regardless, the text of Simon's book provides a particular analysis of the Sub-committee that reads,

> The coalition government was dominated by (or at least relied on) the serried ranks of Conservative MPs largely of the old-fashioned traditional Tory type. Their attitude to education, at least as publically expressed in two extraordinary [Sub-committee] reports published in 1942, ["Looking Ahead" and "A Plan for Youth"] seemed to many more akin to Fascist ideology than to democratic reform (1991, 66).

This statement does reflect 1940s' criticism of the Sub-committee but not Dean's or Harris' subsequent analytical conclusions on the Sub-committee and its Conservative leader, R. A. Butler. Simon's analysis is also discordant as he later notes that, "the chairman of [the Conservative] Sub-Committee [on education] was G. S. Faber, a publisher and not an MP" (1991, 66). Historiographical analysis of Simon's thoughts on the Sub-committee benefits greatly from comparing it to other interpretations.

A close reading of Simon's *Education and the Social Order* also raises some questions about his research methodology, particularly his source "'data-base'." Although the book was not published until 1991, Simon states that he began collecting source material and forming analysis much earlier during his career as an educationalist. He notes in the introduction that from late in 1940, "my wife and I . . . kept quantities of cuttings from both the national and educational press concerning those aspects of educational discussion and action that appeared to us important . . . These cuttings, filed and reorganised with much labour, have provided the spine, or to use the modern idiom, the 'data-base' for this book" (1991, 17). It is not clear if this preliminary work was reassessed in terms of deeper historical analysis later in Simon's career, including the addition of sources outside his personal archive. Simon's reading of the Sub-committee, however, suggests that at least some of this work may have relied too heavily on news reports and secondary sources.

Simon also glosses over plans for further education schemes, an odd choice this time given his own mother's intricate involvement with further education following the 1944 Act. Simon does commend some proposals for further education arguing "important gains . . . recorded for the reform movement" include "the developments of further education" and "'leisure-time occupations'" (1991, 75). Yet sustained analysis of these issues, either within education history, or as developed by the architects of the 1944 Act, is missing. An explanation of this oversight is linked to Simon's underlying historiographical theses: The need for a radical shift toward comprehensive secondary education for all, and the failures of Butler and the architects of the 1944 Act to do so. At the same time that Simon maligns Conservative views on education he salutes the efforts of radical educationalists and the Left to revolutionize English education in secondary and higher education. In *Education and the Social Order* Simon argues that these goals were achieved in the "break-outs" of the Sixties.

In his theoretical apex of postwar educational reform, Simon characterizes the "break-out[s]" in education, catalyzed in part by reactions to the Suez crisis and the Soviet launch of Sputnik in the late 1950s, "as . . . formative, and indeed unique, 'moment[s] of change' within British education" (1991, 221). He goes on to characterize the educational advancements in the 1960s as historical paradigms, a true but perhaps awkward pronouncement by a historian personally involved in promoting, not just writing about, these "break-outs."

Although certainly the 1960s saw transitions in educational trends, such as an increase in the numbers of students attending higher education, and national political actions for comprehensives schools, the long-term historical meanings of these trends are not as clear-cut, radically progressive, or heroic as Simon argues in his analysis. Simon adhered to a more strictly defined secularist and egalitarian interpretation of "secondary education for all." Yet in the 1940s and 1950s, at least, these issues were clouded with the confusion of the immediate postwar situation: Chaos across Europe and in Britain including political conflicts between the West and the Communist East. Intellectual life was often split along these political philosophies but led, as Tony Judt argues, by "postwar ['young'] European intellectuals . . . in a hurry and impatient with compromise"

(2005, 198). A key area glossed over by Marxist historians, for example, was religious culture. This included an indifference to the Christian ethics suggested by the mandate of Religious Education. Lack of attention to religion and Religious Education has now become a glaring gap in late twentieth-century historiography. In regard to the 1944 Act, because Butler and his peers regarded Religious Education as a key aspect of their educational philosophy, ignoring or misunderstanding its significance distorts readings of the 1944 Act.

Yet in *Education and the Social Order*, for example, Simon virtually ignores the mandate for Religious Education in English schools between 1940 and 1990. He briefly discusses it in terms of legislative settlements reached in 1944 and 1988. Nonetheless, his clearest [and longest] statement about Religious Education simply describes the continuation of the dual system after 1944. His conclusions suggest this was nothing but a continuation of a power conspiracy between the churches and the Conservative political system: "A Conservative minister had once again intervened to ensure the continuance of the dual system" (1991, 74). The dual system was maintained, but not simply for the political motivations Simon suggests. His analysis assumes that the continuation of dual control was a victory for the churches and conservative forces, rather than a postsecular reading of the shift from the hard power of the churches to the hard and soft power of education for state welfare. Obviously, with his death in 2002, Simon's own work could not benefit from the hindsight of post-9/11 postsecular thought. Twenty-first century historians, however, may now read Simon's interpretations of the social order and the making of the 1944 Act as secondary and primary sources in the history of education.

Reading Simon's historical work as a primary source suggests his historical interpretations may have contributed to the marginalization of third-way interpretations including Christian-civic humanism. Rather than developing an understanding of moderate reforms that utilized industrial progress tempered by Christianity and traditional national character, following Simon's paradigm shift in the field, many historians of education became focused on Marxist interpretations. Not until late in the twentieth century did the history of education shift to a new lens of historical analysis focused on alternative educational philosophies. Historians began to more closely examine how and where those alternative philosophies made their mark. This investigation led directly to more nuanced interpretations of Butler's 1944 Act and its role as a missing link in social reform that suggested both progressive materialist and a revived "Christian polity" as identified by Jose Harris. Intellectual historian

Harris' nuanced thesis about links between idealist thinking and welfare policies offers clues to follow in state welfare education schemes and identifies key protagonists.

In her work between 1986 and 2003 Harris defines collective intellectual thought on state welfare concepts: "A common language of visionary patriotism and a common sense of national unity" [despite the] "immense diversity of values and goals" (1992, 238). This description has now become a standard interpretation of World War II years. Harris specifies a crucial distinction that remained: a division between progress and reconstruction by means of a "progressive materialism," and that of a revived "Christian polity" (1992, 238-9). This division, however, did not mean that all thinkers took either a secular or a religious path.

In her criticism of Corelli Barnett's *Audit of War*, for example, Harris makes a suggestive statement about Barnett's criticism of Christian thought (1986). She argues that Butler's Conservative Sub-committee on Education proposed educational reform that, "with the sole exception of the emphasis on Christian doctrine . . . was an almost exact replica of the . . . [progressive materialism] . . . Barnett appears to think *should* have been adopted by Britain's wartime planners" (1986, 55-56). This ties to Harris' argument that, "cultural resistance to technological and organizational change had no necessary connection with support for Christianity" (1986, 55). Indeed, the analysis that had been needed and missing was how cultural *acceptance* of technological and organizational change was supported by Christians. This interpretation leads directly to Butler's educational philosophy and the 1944 Act as a proposal for Christian-civic humanism.

Harris' powerful critique of Barnett defended interwar and World War II reformers (including Butler), by arguing that they were not members of a Christian conspiracy, but rather reformers who planned a "spartan, minimalist, safety-net [welfare state]" (1991, 52). Harris' various work on the intellectual background of state welfare intellectuals does not refer to a Pocockian [republican] civic humanism as described in the Introduction. Rather, the language she uses to describe Butler's philosophies fits into a twentieth-century reading of a tradition of "civil society" (2003). She refers specifically to Butler as both a public "supporter of empiricism and material progress," and "privately . . . hanker[ing] after . . . an organic Christian hierarchy" (1987, 240). She makes clear references to and provides evidence for the "search for a 'modernist' reformulation of (or an ethical substitute for) traditional Christianity" in addition to Platonism, as providing "a series of clues, principles and practical nostrums with which to approach the problems of mass, urban, class-based, industrial and imperial civilization" (1992, 124 and 127). Finally, she notes British "idealist" interests in "active citizenship" (1992, 123). These descriptions capture the Christian-civic humanism of Butler as well as his interests in planning for the future using a modern and reformist language and Harris clearly recognizes and helps expose the tradition of idealism in state welfare and civil society as something to which these men contributed.

Harris' vital analysis lies in a broader intellectual, political, and welfare state history yet her conclusions about Butler and the 1944 Act leave some gaps to be filled by not fully deconstructing the contexts and meanings of the civic *and* Christian program suggested by the Conservative Sub-committee on Education. Harris may also underestimate Butler's abilities as well as his educational philosophies—Harris concludes that Butler shied away from legislation of the "idealist" conclusions and proposals that the Conservative Sub-committee on Education proposed, an interpretation this study questions.

By the turn of the twentieth century surprisingly little had been written on the broader historical and cultural meanings of the 1944 Act's religious mandates for the "spiritual [and] moral . . . development of the community," beyond some analyses of the relationships between the churches and the state. Even Callum Brown's more recent work on religion, *Religion and Society in Twentieth-Century Britain,* offered in part as a revision to his *The Death of Christian Britain,* largely disregards Religious Education. Although in *Religion and Society* Brown revises his earlier claims for "the death of Christian Britain" in the 1960s and argues that since 9/11 "religion is back on the agenda" as the first line of his preface, he spends little more than a few lines in the book analyzing the hard and soft power of Religious Education that English schools have possessed—and used—since 1944. The comments and analysis he does make are dispersed throughout 319 pages of text and they are primarily directed at the anticipation of Christian social reformers and clergy, such as Archbishop William Temple, of gaining a foothold for Religious Education through the 1944 religious mandate. Brown makes limited analysis of educational and student responses to Religious Education. For example, Brown suggests that Religious Education was insignificant because it "was clearly not sustaining the interest of the young in the Christian faith" despite the fact that, "religion was bizarrely the only subject that was legislated as compulsory in the curriculum [until 1988]" (2006, 279 and 289). This statement may now be regarded as an ingenuous argument on several levels.

Schoolchildren are notoriously not interested in many of their school lessons, which is why debates over the rights and responsibilities of parentalism in education exist. Brown's own definitions of "Christian faith" are called into question as well. The "discursive Christianity" he identifies in *The Death of Christian Britain* (2001), until a sudden drop-off in the early 1960s, has been critiqued for its limited definitions of what religion, spirituality, and faith meant and how they were understood by ordinary people. Thus, scholars such as Jeremy Morris find Brown's definition of religion limited. Morris argues that Brown, "acknowledges ['things'] at one level but refuses to consider [them] significant" (2003, 969-70). This extends to Brown's dismissal of the educational mandate for Religious Education.

Tweaking Morris' argument slightly, a noticeably missing piece of analysis, considering that Brown alludes to the subject at least five times in his 2006 book, is the role of Religious Education in English society since 1944. Brown fails to offer any discussion of how and why state-mandated Religious Education developed and was put into law in 1944. Given that Brown argues for a resurgence of British Christian culture in the 1940s and 1950s, he spends curiously little time on the development or effects of the mandate for Religious Education and worship. In part, this is related to Brown's focus on a reanalysis of secularization and his thesis that shifts periodization of these trends in modern British history. Brown's claim for the "death of Christian Britain" in the 1960s is vital in religious historiography. Nonetheless, Religious Education and collective worship in schools remained mandatory post-1960 and influenced students and society. Indeed, only a year after the publication of Brown's 2006 monograph, the Office for Standards in Education, UK, (Ofsted) confirmed this by arguing, "The notions, common until recently, that religion was quietly declining and Religious Education had little relevance to modern life now look naïve" (2007). It was time to ask how Religious Education did affect students and culture.

Brown is not alone in glossing over these issues. Historians' now noticeable lack of attention to Religious Educational culture was rooted in narrow focus on historiographical trends including a church-state thesis based on readings of a partnership between the state and the church to maintain dual control in education. Historians' foci also addressed analyses of disputes and consensus among Christian denominations in terms of the content of Religious Education. These institutional and political analyses out-numbered cultural analyses, with a few notable exceptions. Two theories for these oversights are suggested, one cultural and one political. First, mandatory Religious Education was not regarded as historically significant in the 1940s and 1950s because, in Brown's estimation, it fit into his depiction of increased religiosity in the immediate postwar years. By the 1960s it had changed to a Religious Education of multiculturalism and global politics (i.e. a secularized Religious Education). Thus, because it could be read as a trend that fit into left-wing, if not secularizing, politics, it was an issue that could be glossed over.

A relatively small number of significant studies, including those aforementioned by Charmian Cannon and Harris, have better illustrated how progressive intellectual thought from Christian intellectuals became linked to state welfare reform in the 1940s. Cannon's 1964 article is an important early article in this vein. Cannon analyzes the cultural pressures on Religious Education and legislation as well as the religious convictions of the architects of the 1944 Act. She also examines the pro-religiosity of politicians on both sides of the aisle. The state, under a Religious Education mandate, gained hard power to teach an Anglo-Christian philosophy to a captive audience of students and the soft power to imbue English education with Christian ethics. The churches maintained soft power in education through their advisory roles in creating agreed syllabi and contemporary curriculum framework to imbue society with Christian themes and ideals for commonweal. Matthew Grimley also contributes to work on Christian intellectuals whose work was crucial to a Christian-civic humanist educational philosophy (2003).

Twenty-first century interpretations must also grapple with the effects of mandated Religious Education in English culture and society because the 1988 Education Act reaffirmed mandatory Religious Education and added a "broadly Christian" identification to the legislation (5). Religious Education remains a compulsory subject in the twenty-first century. Trends, statistics, and the continued mandate of 1944 education policies in England raise questions, then, about historical wisdom that describes the postwar decades in England—even the Sixties—as ones of singular and lasting radical reform and secularization. Jay Winter's argument in *Sites of Memory, Sites of Mourning* applies to a longer historical period,

> That some aspects of twentieth-century [culture] are revolutionary goes without saying . . . What is more difficult to accept is that 'modernism', more a temperament than a set of fixed beliefs, left behind as neatly and surgically as some scholars suggest the host of images and conventions derived from eighteenth and nineteenth century religious, romantic, or classical traditions . . . To array the past in such a way is to invite distortion by losing a sense of its messiness, its non-linearity, its vigorous and stubbornly visible incompatibilities (2014, 4).

Interpretations of the 1944 Act often glossed over the Christian philosophies that gilded its practical civic ideals. Renewed examinations of secondary and further education help fill gaps in the historiography of the 1944 Act as state welfare. A variety of ideas, means, and methods for viable secondary and further education programs and choices were offered for the vast majority of students who would not attend university-prep grammar schools or specialized technical schools.

As a variety of scholars have argued in relation to English educational philosophies, socio-cultural biases against more practical and informal forms of education remain rooted in English culture. Nonetheless, secondary modern and technical schools served well over a million English citizens. The long-term results of their education remain a mystery, as do the long-term effects of mandated Religious Education. In any case, it is clear that the history of education in twentieth-century England remains a field where more work can be done. The study at hand begins with examination of three Christian-civic humanists: Butler, Clarke, and Mannheim.

CHAPTER THREE

CHRISTIAN-CIVIC HUMANISTS

> Such [a modern] age is not merely creative. It is also dissolvent. And just because the pace is so swift, we are not always careful to see that it is only what we no longer need that is lost. Often we throw the baby out with the bath-water. Sometimes we even throw the baby out and retain the bath-water.
> —R. A. Butler, "The 1944 Act Seen against the Pattern of the Times," 1952

R. A. Butler

A leader in a progressive wing of interwar Conservatives, R. A. Butler designed and promoted a New Conservatism which was anti-Socialist but not anti-progressive. Butler's New Conservatism was presented as a philosophy, rather than a political ideology or platform. As a philosophy it served as part of a broader intellectual trend: an idealism that contributed to social policy decisions for state welfare. Butler possessed a keen intellectual and political drive which allowed him to serve in a variety of high government posts during his lengthy political career, and this background contributed greatly to the political and educational philosophies that shaped his best known work—the creation and passage of the 1944 Education Act.

Butler was born in 1902 to a traditionally Conservative, religiously-minded, and intellectual family. During the early interwar years he served as a Cambridge don before he entered the House of Commons in 1929 at the age of twenty-six. He served as Under-Secretary of State for India (1932-1937), as well as Parliamentary Secretary to the Ministry of Labour (1937-1938), and Under-Secretary of State for Foreign Affairs (1938-1941).

This work contributed to his progressive New Conservative philosophy—a philosophy distinctive enough to gain the moniker "Butlerite Toryism." Butler's Toryism represented a forward-thinking wing of the Conservative party separate from other neo-conservative movements. Butler's political and diplomatic work on Commonwealth issues and foreign affairs, combined with the practical realities of modern labor, drove his interest in creating progressive and reformist legislation.

Butler's intellectual work and policy proposals thus embraced conservative and reformist issues and his Conservative, Christian, and academic milieux gave him a strong basis for the Christian-civic humanism that characterized Butler Toryism. By the late 1930s, Butler served as Chair of the Conservative Central Education Committee, giving him the opportunity to further develop his intellectual and political interests into educational policies.

Ironically, however, Butler's earliest work on educational philosophy and as chair of the Conservative Party's Central Education Committee and Postwar Problems Committee has not been fully appreciated as part and parcel of his intellectual and political work for the 1944 Education Act. Even his biographer, Anthony Howard, argued that Butler concocted his plans for educational reform "[on] holiday [in] isolation," after his appointment to the Board of Education (Howard 1987, 114). To the contrary, Butler, from at least the late 1930s, was deeply and publically interested in issues of creating a Christian-civic educational philosophy. His early ideas promoted thinking to engender consensus reforms that synthesized traditional values with modern idioms. This explicitly included religious idioms. The work of his colleagues did as well. In 1940 a Board of Education civil servant argued in "Policy and Planning for Postwar Education" that if education officials did not move boldly to reform education, "others will be asked to design the 'new Jerusalem'" ("Education after the War"). These "devotees at the shrine of progress," as Butler would come to call them in a 1942 speech to the National Union of Teachers (NUT), fervently believed that England could remain a glorious, sovereign, and Christian island despite the sea of secular evils and moral depravity that threatened to flood its plains. Educationalists believed this future could be shaped by a reformed educational system. Specifically, enforced Religious Education, alongside a restructured school system, could serve as a panacea for the plagues of global conflict as well as the fluctuations of modernity. Education reform could build links between politically—and socially—motivated educational divides to restore a community spirit to the industrialized but democratic nation-state.

In 1938 Butler's ideology was laid out in a political education booklet, *A National Faith: By a Modern Conservative.* Although Butler wrote only the introduction to the main text written by C. J. M. Alport, his biographer argues that Butler "was in every sense [the publication's] midwife" including passing it through Conservative party bureaucracy and securing Faber & Faber as publisher (Howard 1987, 81). This document reveals an early public version of Butler's plans to create an educational system infused with specific traits of English history and culture as a means to re-inspire and re-invigorate the English community. Because Butler embraced both progress and tradition he named only a "modern Conservative" as author of *A National Faith*—a move he believed represented synthesis and diplomacy, rather than antithesis and revolution, as a better reflection of the English spirit.

Butler was a consummate diplomat and knew that to be successful his efforts must be practical and popular. He argued in the introduction to *A National Faith*,

> Political education has for many years been grievously handicapped by the lack of cheap, concise, and readable books . . . [t]here [is] . . . a really urgent need for the sort of book which could be easily read and yet would meet the demand for up-to-date information and thought on modern political problems (7).

A National Faith clearly spelled out Butler's Tory "political education" goals including "stimulating an interest in public affairs" (7). Butler stressed that his group's goal was to make their work accessible to "the average student of current affairs" (7). He also emphasized the importance of political education to civil society, including encouragement of active and participatory citizenship, democratic rights and responsibilities, individualism, and a spirit of public good. Thus, Butler Toryism insisted on progressive social reform and a contemporary civic humanism. The closing lines of the first chapter of *A National Faith*, "The Challenge of the Times," argued,

> The world in which we live to-day is not [Prime Minister Benjamin] Disraeli's [nineteenth-century] world and we cannot hope to answer the challenge by invoking voices from that dead, if glorious past. If Conservatism is going to justify itself in the eyes of our new democracy . . . it must answer that challenge firmly and clearly in the spirit of the times in which it is made (19-20).

At the same time, Butler and his cohort believed some English traditions could still serve commonweal. Butler's interests in Christianity as a theme for social progress, for example, also began to emerge in *A National Faith*. British democracy was described as "a political system in which national unity is provided by some all-embracing loyalty," and Christianity was described as "the greatest" of four institutions of democracy (62 and 70.) Butler's third-way politics were revealed: belief in progress and tradition to synthesize a democratic commonweal rather than a purely laissez-faire or a secular socialist paradigm.

Butler continued to address issues of political education and progressive reform in his work. His 1939 address, "The Future of Political Education," is one of the clearest of his statements on these issues. This speech, when read with an eye on Butler's intellectual and reformist mind-set, depicts the further development of Christian-civic educational philosophy from its early form in *A National Faith*. Butler continued to describe a democratic public good that took individual autonomy under consideration, yet understood the modern necessity for national guidance in areas of social policy such as education.

In "The Future of Political Education," Butler argued that the "general objective" of "political education" was "to fit people the better for politics" as part of a wider project to adapt "to the new order of things" engendered by the "great world events" that surrounded contemporary society (1-2). He further argued, "we must try to inspire ['a new generation'] with the ideals in which we believe ['service and patriotism'] and to impart the necessary knowledge upon which a sound political judgment can be based" (1-3). In a time of flux, Butler was developing an educational philosophy that would employ "national character" (6) and English tradition for commonweal objectives. The speech did not mention Christianity or Religious Education specifically as the bases for this traditional culture. It did, however, contain language that pointed toward Butler's spiritual beliefs. He spoke of creating "the ['right'] attitude inspired by our wish to create a good life in its real sense rather than one based purely on materialism" (9). A "[real] good life" was put in direct opposition to materialism. Thus Butler championed civic and spiritual traditions as inherent to a "good life." Contemporary English readers would have known that spirituality was synonymous with Christianity.

Butler's plans did not propose radical changes but rather reformist shifts in education. Butler not only had a respect for tradition but realized that reform in England must conform to its unique national character of sober compromises rather than rash revolutionary actions. A reformed English system of education would then differ from the radically nationalized or comprehensive systems put in place in other European nation-states. Nazi Germany and the Soviet Union were crucial examples of extremist reforms in education and society that proved problematic. These movements pointed toward hardline secular and statist schooling and society. Butler made clear in his 1939 speech that the Nazi educational system, specifically, loomed as a sinister example of the moral dangers, yet practical effectiveness, of those systems (8).

Although Butler's biographer reports that Butler had shown an interest in the origins of the Hitler Youth Movement as a national and "public spirit" drive for youth service and further education, his interest disappeared once the totalitarian nature of Nazi Germany revealed itself (Howard 1987, 76). In "The Future of Political Education" Butler decried Nazi attempts at "political education," as too "extreme" because of the overwhelming state control the Nazis attempted (8). He argued in the speech for an increased state role in education based on "practical idealism" but without "the complete invasion by the State of the Curriculum" (7-8).

Butler's goals for the public good also included progressive ideals related to labor and social conditions as outlined in "The Future of Political Education:" Working classes were necessary to the well-being of the nation. Butler suggested that those who benefit from this labor had a responsibility to those who did the work (1939, 9). Butler recommended investigation and reform of "the weaknesses of our economic and industrial system" (3). Butler's vision for "human planning" was decidedly anti-socialist, but it was also against "Americanization," or "[a] materialist basis of society, which took the form in the U.S.A. of the pursuit of the dollar" (3). Rather, Butler imagined a system that could promote economic growth and enterprise, while maintaining a core system of values and ethics. Such a system could serve as a steering wheel during the rapid forward drive in technology and industrialism that Britain must take in order to raise domestic living standards and remain economically viable and a world leader. Rather than Soviet Communism or American liberalism, Butler looked for a specifically English method to engender economic growth but also provide moderation and social justice. State support and planning served as a means to create both attributes. He argued,

> We must . . . show by conduct and action that we are not merely a party hitched to the chariot wheels of property and finance . . . Our quest will be a voyage of discovery to find a new setting for all that is best in the words 'freedom' and 'democracy,' and we shall lead our crusade against over-industrialisation and over-intellectualism (1939, 5).

Butler believed the national character of the English was far better than this and English temperament could be rekindled in political and social policies. He argued in his 1939 "Political Education" that the nation's "attitude to State Education," as well as "education in citizenship," required careful examination and reform to create a system between a purely liberal education and a purely political education (5-7). Butler's vision was a synthesis between the two based on "practical idealism," but steering clear of an "inhuman conception of Economic Man" (8). Rather, through a synthesis of both traditional and "new values which outweigh material interests," England could shape an educational system "to inspire [people] with the ideals in which we believe and to impart . . . knowledge . . . [for] sound political judgment" (1, 3, and 8). In sum, by 1939, Butler possessed and promoted a clear educational philosophy grounded in centrist politics: active and patriotic citizenship secured with both traditional and progressive means; the need for and worth of workers; strong moral and spiritual traditions; and a balance between England's commonweal claims and the rights of individuals.

As a diplomat, Butler wisely sought both party and wider national discourse on his proposals for political education and state welfare. This began with popular and political work on civics and education. Fortuitously, while his background in politics and government made him politic, he also easily found like-minded colleagues. His interest in educational issues paralleled that of other interwar thinkers including educationalists. Fred Clarke, director of the Institute of Education at the University of London between 1936 and 1945, for example, worked on similar policy proposals and would eventually serve as one of Butler's colleagues.

Fred Clarke

Clarke was closely associated with other English educationalists and policy-makers during the interwar years. He remains a noted, but under-analyzed, Christian intellectual and educationalist. Examination of his work reveals that he was not only well-connected but widely influential. Respected educationalists such as Gary McCulloch and Colin McCaig identify his vision of education and social change as one of the three key versions "of a specifically English tradition in education . . . [in the twentieth century]" (2002, 238). This educational philosophy converged on several key points: The unification of the educational system; a synthesis between liberal and vocational forms of education; curriculum relevant to the modern era; increased state involvement in education; and increased social cohesion through education by emphasis of shared Christian spirituality. Clarke developed much of this educational philosophy during the interwar period in work written while employed abroad in the Commonwealth but it was published for an English audience.

Born to a farming family in Oxfordshire in 1880, Clarke embarked on his impressive journey as an educationalist in 1899 after receiving a Queen's Scholarship to attend Oxford University Day Training College.

He studied history and received his teacher training and in 1906 became a professor of education at Hartley University College, Southampton. From 1911-1929, he held the Chair of Education at the University of Cape Town, South Africa and then served as Professor of Education at McGill University in Montreal, Canada (1929-34). Although Clarke served abroad during the early interwar years, he influenced English educational circles with his 1923 *Essays in the Politics of Education.*

While working in South Africa, Clarke argued for "the need for a philosophy" in English and Commonwealth education related to "religion and a religious attitude" (1923, 1). His *Essays in the Politics of Education* responded directly to revolution in Russia and "our own Great War" (1). Clarke argued, in a statement worth quoting at length for the various themes it raises,

> Many signs are apparent of the beginnings of the new synthesis of our educational ideas, but as yet it is the disintegration of the old that most strikes the eye. Declining belief in older methods and older aims, not only in education but on all sides of the common life; the disappearance of old landmarks; dark portents like the upheaval in Russia; the decay of older political, economic, and religious faiths; have reduced us to a state of lost bewilderment which is reflected strongly in the comparative aimlessness and want of strong, clear, *meaning*, which now characterize so much of our education (5).

Clarke, like Butler, believed society should evolve rather than revolutionize. Evolution was based on synthesis: compromise between tradition and reform without which he argued in his *Essays*, "the whole effort may pass into aimlessness and meaningless" (1923, 1). In addition, Clarke believed that education was a humanistic and spiritual endeavor. As such, his essays argued that education and educational reform must be based on unifying forces to guide its development. For Clarke, education was intricately intertwined with the guiding light of spirituality. He argued, "Education as a whole in all its aspects and in its relationship to life is unintelligible except as a progressive revelation of what we mean both in belief and practice when we speak of the Eternal . . . To know God and to enjoy him forever" (2). Religion was an organic system of faith used to navigate the world. Clarke's thinking was similar to John Milton's thoughts in *Of Education* to transcend the mere "commonwealth," and "reconstitute . . . the solid thing" (1644, 407-8). Although Clarke drew on Milton as an inspiration in the history of English commonweal principles, Clarke did not believe Milton went far enough in his soul-searching (1940, 67).

Although education and religion were deeply metaphysical issues for Clarke, he was also practical-minded. Thus he worked to reconcile educational philosophy with progressive and practical reforms to benefit twentieth-century English society. Clarke realized that contemporary generations faced socio-economic challenges far removed from earlier visions of a Christian commonwealth. Clarke identified "the established industrial order" as one of the "most formidable obstacles that stand[s] in the way of [contemporary] synthesis" (1923, 19). Clarke recognized the historical divisions between ideals of "liberal or vocational" education (1923, 48-84). Nevertheless, he argued that the "antithesis" of these two forms of education must be reanalyzed in both historical and contemporary thought. Contemporary educationalists, Clarke argued in his 1923 *Essays*, must consider the value of both liberal and vocational education and synthesize them to create more meaningful contemporary education.

Clarke also recognized the tensions the Industrial Revolution had wrought on both liberal and vocational education, such as the slow but steady disintegration of the apprenticeship system which he argued symbolized an earlier transcendence of cultural-vocational distinctions. Traditionally apprenticeship had involved extra-economic connections between a master and apprentice resulting in a system with links to broader structures of culture and community. The break-down of this system had created disjointed academic and vocational education. Clarke argued that by the early twentieth century "the old conception of a socially exclusive liberal education [was] faced with a demand for complete transformation, and the new conception of a popular education [was] growing up with no clear guiding principle at all" (1923, 55). Contemporary culture, Clarke argued, must once again transcend what he called a "cultural-vocational" divide:

> What is wanted is not a separate core for Leisure and Work in distinction, but an importation of the spirit of Leisure into Work. For Leisure is not a period of time, not even a certain type of external occupation; it is an attitude of mind towards whatever one may be doing. It is the attitude of a free man who finds means to express the fullness of his nature, even when constrained by hard, economic necessity . . . The education we seek is one that will literally turn the very chains of servitude into the habiliments of Freedom (1923, 66-67).

Clarke formulated his philosophy of education as a means toward a new synthesis of liberal and vocational education designed and balanced for modern England, a democratic and capitalist country where daily life necessitated liberal and vocational training.

Thus, Clarke's educational philosophy, like Butler's, reflected English traditions and the realities of the world around him. An educational system, argued Clarke, should prepare people for the life of work that an industrialized economic system made virtually mandatory. Yet, he suggested, Christian philosophies and ethics, offered alongside this modern education, could provide a humanizing instinct and a source of spiritual life. Transcending the "cultural-vocational" distinction in education meant that education must encompass liberal and religious education as well as vocational education.

In 1935, Clarke returned to England, where he first served as Advisor to Overseas Students (1935) and then as Director (as well as a professor) at the Institute of Education, University of London (1936-45). He also worked on another volume of educational philosophy, *Education and Social Change: An English Interpretation,* published in 1940. In this work, Clarke further developed the educational philosophy set out in his 1923 *Essays*. He argued that current conflicts linked to Communist and Fascist movements, "appear . . . in many forms within the social structure of every civilized people [and] are . . . *historical*, the impact of history itself upon our generation" (3). Clarke was also quite certain that the problems which faced English education were "sociological, rather than pedagogic" (5). Clarke believed society must shape education, not the other way around. Yet Clarke remained adamant that evolution, not revolution, was the answer.

He argued, "the English educational tradition [can] adapt itself without undue friction or shattering to the demands of a changed order" (1940, 1). The reformist spirit needed, Clarke argued, was one of liberty but with an emphasis on individual educational liberty: "That is, in relation to the aptitudes of pupils," not based on maintaining castes or classes or in creating upward social mobility (63). Only a synthesis of education for work and leisure could guide industrialized man toward a reconstitution of what Milton had called "the solid thing" and that Clarke had rephrased as "the need for a philosophy."

This task would not be easy, Clarke realized, but he believed the necessary turning points had been reached. He argued, "It is society at large that will have to decide the issue and there appears to be not much doubt what the decision will be" (1940, 63). He outlined the necessary social changes in the 1940 document: "A changed attitude towards State action," meaning that private citizens and institutions would accept increased state control over education (65). Clarke argued that this had begun, but that "at the boundary lines of schools of the upper levels [public schools and universities], it stops short" (66). This represented a criticism, not support for, the public and largely autonomous university systems. Finally, Clarke cited wider acceptance of "State action" in education and "the development of a popular philosophy of education" as the "most relevant" examples of changes needed in "basic [English] attitudes" toward education (66). This popular philosophy and state action, he argued, would not be a revolutionary transition from traditional English attitudes, but would serve "to preside over the process of unifying the values of culture and usefulness" (66).

Clarke argued in his 1940 *Education and Social Change* that English-Christian traditions could serve as the cultural foundation for the revival of the nation, not to mention set an example for "Western liberal tradition[s]" (3-4). He noted the catalyst of military conflict, "If the furnace of war serves to mould and establish that faith in us, we shall not have gone through it in vain" (70). Although he (like Butler) did not refer directly to Christianity, as his book's General Preface did, Clarke referred to "the nature of social cohesion" in profoundly religious terms (66-70). In a series of questions and answers, he argued that English society should "continue to cohere" and that this can only be achieved "by life and sound education and the grace of God" (67-70). The reason, Clarke argued, for social cohesion was "so religious in expression . . . It is: for the making of souls" (67). This "social cohesion," although easily translated as "religion," was much more than an institutionalized, church-based religious culture: it was the soul of the nation, and its spirit reflected the national character. Thus, even in his materialist philosophies, Clarke turned to religion for answers about how to serve a commonweal.

Leading educationalists regarded Clarke's *Education and Social Change* as influential. Its publisher, the *Christian News-Letter*, stated in the introduction: "[This volume as part of a series is meant] to assist thought upon the relation of the Christian faith to present problems" making Clarke's underlying Christian philosophy crystal clear (3-4). Clarke himself argued that, "I have been given reason to believe that [the book] had some influence on the course of events, helping as it did to guide and crystallize [a] body of [educational] opinion . . ." (Mitchell 1967, 166).[4] While limiting his structural advice to "a broad indication of the main framework," Clarke argued against an expansion of the elementary system as an organization flawed with "increasingly obsolete 'class' associations" (1940, 49). Rather, he urged focus on reconstruction of a secondary system as "one whole design planned to cover the

[4] Frank W. Mitchell's *Sir Fred Clarke: Master Teacher* includes "two hitherto Unpublished Memoranda," one by Fred Clarke, c. 1930 and one by Karl Mannheim, c. 1948, in Appendix B, 161-169.

requirements of the entire adolescent population" (1940, 50). He noted, however, that, "due regard for English concern for a wide diversity of school types," as well as the "freedom of individual schools," must be taken into consideration (49). These socio-political concerns tied his earlier philosophical statements to a holistic Christian-civic humanism.

Clarke's approach toward cultural and social educational philosophy helped cement his relationship with a key interwar sociologist: Karl Mannheim. Indeed, in his close study of Clarke, *Sir Fred Clarke: Master Teacher*, Frank W. Mitchell notes that Clarke, himself, brought Mannheim to the Institute of Education on part-time loan from the London School of Economics (Mitchell 1967). Clarke also recommended Mannheim's appointment to a chair at the Institute and promoted his sociological theories to friends, colleagues, and politicians. Mannheim, a well-connected and influential European sociologist, provided a critical sociological perspective to English Christian-civic humanism.

Karl Mannheim

Mannheim was born in Budapest in 1894 and was educated in Budapest, Berlin, Paris, and Freiburg. A friend and teacher, Georg Lukács, offered Mannheim a position at the Hungarian Soviet. After the collapse of the government in 1919, Mannheim moved to Germany and held academic posts at Heidelberg and Frankfurt until the first National Socialist enactments in 1933 suspended him from his posts. He then fled to England in 1933 as an exile from Germany. Already a noted European intellectual, he was invited to take a position at the London School of Economics and quickly found a place within the English intelligentsia. In 1938-39 Mannheim was invited to join an English Christian intellectual group, the Moot. Mannheim met Clarke during the group's meetings in 1939. Soon after, Clarke brought Mannheim in as faculty at the Institute of Education where he became a popular and influential colleague.

English intellectuals, educationalists, and politicians, however, made their mark on Mannheim as well. His "Third Way" sociological theories, especially those concerning "planning for freedom," and "militant democracy," reached the apex of their development during his years in England. As outlined in his 1943 *Diagnosis of our Time*, Mannheim's argument for third-way politics was based on what he called "militant democracy" (6-10). Mannheim argued for a blending of tradition and new leadership; a middle-ground of "militant" political maneuvers that were more active than the "neutrality" of "laissez-faire Liberalism," but without "strait-jacket social organization" of dictators. Rather, Mannheim called for a renewed sense of democratic values as a basic consensus between citizens within a given society (9-10).

In the case of England, Mannheim was also willing to consider English Christianity, in addition to secular democratic values, as an agreed set of social values. Nevertheless, Mannheim challenged English Christian thinkers, such as his friends and colleagues in the Moot, to consider carefully the form and substance Christianity might take within "Planning for Freedom" (1944, 109). Here he outlined several key considerations: the "generally accepted values must be based upon tacit or explicit consensus;" these basic values, or "virtues," could "be brought home through education and social influence;" but "recommendations" rather than "force" were best advised (1944, 118-21 and Chapter VII). Mannheim argued that a "basic consensus" could be enforced but that room should be left for "individual creed [and] free experimentation"(120). This suggests principles linked to both republican and democratic political philosophies in maintaining rule of law and the voice of the people.

Mannheim revised his sociological theories for English society after his contact with various English intellectuals with specific reference to the Moot. Indeed, his *Diagnosis of our Times,* although not published until 1943, revealed the debt he felt owed to British Christian intellectuals who had helped him reshape and redefine his theories in the late interwar and early war years. Mannheim's footnote to chapter VII, "Towards a New Social Philosophy: A Challenge to Christian Thinkers by a Sociologist," dedicated the chapter to "a group of British friends, Christian thinkers," (109). Analysis of Mannheim's work indicates this reference is to the Moot, although Mannheim did not refer to the group by name.

Written for a popular audience, *Diagnosis of Our Time* accepted the kind of "political education" Butler promoted. It provided, as the title suggested, a diagnosis of the World War II-era societies, comparing the mistakes of Fascist mass societies with the promise democratic mass societies held if developed with humanistic principles. The book focused on education and English society in particular, with sections on "the problem of youth," "the changing features of modern educational practice," and "Christianity in the Age of Planning," reflecting contemporary concerns of English politicians, educationalists, and Christian intellectuals such as Butler and Clarke. Specifically, Mannheim argued that contemporary education must integrate itself more closely with society, work to develop "the wholeness of the person," and move away from overly-specialized academic teaching methods which "neutralize[d] learning" (59-79). Rather, Mannheim went on, education should be geared toward developing "social awareness"—critical and philosophical thinking necessary to citizens in a "progressive democracy." Progressive politicians, Christian educationalists, and sociological theory—clearly symbolized by Butler, Clarke, and Mannheim—were coalescing to provide a panacea for the time: educational reform and reconstruction within a Christian-civic philosophy.

Despite this intellectual ferment and Butler's political determination to push ahead with educational reform, the crises of the war meant that he, his Board, and their intellectual colleagues had to walk a fine line between pushing ahead with their educational reform projects and satisfying Prime Minister Churchill's vital concerns for military action supported by domestic peace. Butler walked this line with grace and poise. Reformist, yet a patriotic diplomat, Butler saw his position as the President of the Board of Education as an opportunity both to promote his developing political and educational philosophies and aid in England's ideological struggle from the domestic front. Beyond Butler's political and intellectual cohorts, contemporary educational research, such as that published in the London County Council's 1941 "Religious Education," promoted reform efforts that melded traditional culture—including religious education—with progressive educational proposals to benefit the nation. Butler believed he could skillfully synthesize the demands of church leaders, politicians, and educationalists into agreeable compromise. This compromise advocated an education bill based on Christian-civic humanism. Butler's World War II domestic battle would be to turn reformist educational philosophies and proposals into viable legislation that would strengthen English minds, bodies, and spirit without creating controversy in a time of national crisis.

CHAPTER FOUR

RECONSTRUCTING EDUCATION

> Upon the education of the people of this country the fate of this country depends.
> —Prime Minister Benjamin Disraeli, as quoted in R. A. Butler's 1943 White Paper on Education Reconstruction.

The political climate of the years surrounding World War II compelled R. A. Butler to pursue reform and legislation cautiously and often behind the scenes of Prime Minister Churchill's directives for the Board of Education. Butler argued that Churchill's vision for the Board of Education during the war amounted to little more than war-time issues such as evacuations and bombed schools and disciplinary and paternalistic actions such as "smacking children's bottoms and blowing their noses" (1971, 108). Butler, however, believed diplomacy and personal and professional contact with "devotees at the shrine of progress" could engender diplomatic discussion about educational reform and solidify proposals for legislation. James Chuter Ede, Parliamentary Secretary at the Board of Education, and Butler's right-hand man at the time, noted in his diary that Butler expressed some anxiety about going behind Churchill's back on educational reforms, stating, "[Butler] said that M. [*sic*] had stated that we might get a measure of educational reform within 3 years. Did I think he was morally justified in pursuing negotiations without [Churchill's] consent to a Bill?" (Chuter Ede 1987, 45). Chuter Ede gave an affirmation in favor of their moral justification. Official and public rhetoric supported Butler's goals for progressive reform in Religious Education, including diplomatic negotiations with the politically-powerful Church. Moreover, it seemed general educational reforms could be welcomed. Whatever his anxieties, Butler began setting the foundation for new legislation in stone immediately after he had settled in as head of the Board of Education.

Butler had entered Education during the extremely tense summer of 1941. During Butler's first months in office the British continued to stand virtually alone against the Germans, amid fears that German plans to invade the British Isles would be carried out. The fears and anxieties of 1941 affected domestic policies including education. In autumn 1941, for example, Churchill determined fuller mobilization for the war effort was necessary and suggested requiring male youth, except those exempt by their involvement with necessary war industries and full-time education, to register for cadet training. Although this move was counterproductive to the Board of Education officials' aims for a youth services system, wartime concerns took precedence. Board of Education officials, however, realized cadet training was administrative and temporary. The Board's main goal remained development of systematic, yet liberal, youth services that could be linked to reforms for the postwar educational system (Rhodes 1939 and Gresh 1940).

Butler clearly understood that a rush to legislation during the war would be foolish. In a letter to Churchill dated September 12, 1941, he had initially proposed forming a Joint Select Committee to carefully examine educational reform proposals. In the letter Butler argued that a Joint Select Committee, as a "body before which the points of view not only of purely educational, but also of wider national interests could be represented," "would be a forum worthy of the issues involved." This was an indication of Butler's interests in using both expert opinion and broader national opinion to construct new legislation. The formation of such a committee, Butler's letter stated, would also allow the Board to test the views of the public as well as to alleviate a potential "dogfight" in Parliament, before submitting an Education Bill. In his 1941 letter to Churchill, Butler argued with the tactful, yet direct, tone that characterized his work:

> The procedure suggested is designed to avoid trespassing too far on the ground of political or sectarian antagonisms just now, while yet providing a method of harnessing the spirit of the times to the cause of social reform. We should be showing the world that we have the urge and vitality, not only to save ourselves and civilization, but also to build for the future.

Butler's memoir states that Churchill rejected the idea for a Joint Committee in the same way he rejected educational reform, fearing it would lead to a resurgence of bitter debates during years the nation desperately needed internal consensus in its fight against external enemies (1971). Butler refused, he recalls in his memoir, to let Churchill's disinterest in real educational progress during the war stop his own plans because he believed that "education [reform was] a prime factor in reconstruction" (108). The proof was in the pudding, including, for example, the 1941 report, "Religious Education," from the London County

Council. The Council's Chief Inspector argued in the report that London children's general education, and specifically their Religious Education, had been disturbed by the war (6-7). Nonetheless, the Chief Inspector reported that children evacuated to the country were experiencing increased levels of education, spirituality, and religiosity due to the more intimate, natural, and traditional life they encountered in pastoral England (6-7). Rural life, he argued, including its traditional religious links, was rejuvenating the English spirit of these slum dwellers (6-7). Such research supported Butler's domestic call to arms for educational reform as part of the war effort and recovery.

By October 1941, in his capacity as the Conservative Central Committee Chair on Postwar Problems, Butler created several sub-committees with which to deal with various issues; one such committee focused on education. Led by Geoffrey Faber, with Fred Clarke in an advisory position, the Conservative Sub-committee on Education served as a surrogate for the Joint Committee Churchill had vetoed. Other notable members of Butler's sub-committees included: Karl Mannheim, T. S. Eliot, and Walter Oakeshott.[5] The Sub-committee on Education worked diligently to produce two concurrent interim reports: "Looking Ahead: Educational Aims" focused on the "two-way character of education" as both a service to individual students and "the cause of community" and "the Religious Factor in Education" (1942, 2). The 1942 "A Plan for Youth" report addressed youth services and further education. In "Educational Aims" the Sub-committee argued,

> No distinction of value can or should be drawn between different types of 'post-primary' education. The scholar, the philosopher, the artist, the scientist, the engineer, the farm-worker, and the artisan are equally necessary types of citizens. But each must learn not to despise, but to admire each other (36).

Along this philosophical vein, Butler organized other sub-committees to work on "Looking Ahead" projects: "Demobilisation and Resettlement," with an eye on "national training and rehabilitation" for vital postwar positions including "Agricultural Reconstruction" which addressed modern agricultural education and research and emphasized higher and further educational opportunities for demobilized soldiers, future workers, and commonweal.

---

[5] Conservative Sub-Committee on Education, 1942-45 records are held at Oxford, Bodleian Library, Conservative Party Archive.

The Sub-committee on Education's "Educational Aims" had initiated this line of thinking: "It has become a matter of life and death that the nation should command the service of all its citizens, high and low, and that this service should be not only willing, but efficient—far more efficient than it has ever been in the past" (1942, 6). This attitude reflected continued anxiety about demographic decline in relation to an overproduction of professional workers at the expense of the industrial, agricultural, and other practical trades and specific fears of postwar shortages of labor. Without a newly-trained population of workers with practical skills, the ageing of the contemporary work force could harm British industry. The Conservative Sub-committee on Education, as well as members of both houses of Parliament and educationalists such as Clarke, made pointed references to these problems and anxieties.

The Sub-committee's second interim report, the 1942 "A Plan for Youth," stated as part of its main purpose "to seek to establish sound foundations for the measures of national reconstruction . . . when victory has been won" (2). Although this interim report came under political fire for its suggestions of compulsory youth services and its allegedly overt nationalism, its philosophical basis supported ideals of restoring a civic humanism to the nation as well as crossing cultural-vocational divides illustrated by this statement:

> By acquiring . . . membership [in the proposed Federation of Youth] . . . [members] will be helped to understand their individual importance to the body politic, as junior citizens who have emerged from the status of children [at the school-leaving age of 14] into the status of youth, and are now and increasingly capable of doing real things in a real grown-up world (1942, 11).

"A Plan for Youth" argued for guidance for these young cohorts in a variety of capacities, including "training of the body," "training of character," and "training of the mind," both as service to the youth as individuals and as a service to the community. Youth services thus would benefit the nation and serve as a means to help alleviate perceived problems of increased juvenile delinquency related to "indictable offenses" laid out in the Children and Young Persons Act of 1933 and offenses committed during the World War II such as the looting of bombed houses and teenage blackout gang violence. In addition, the report argued, in language that echoed its earlier statements, "the schoolboy, the farm worker, the miner, and the factory hand should be made aware of the part that their work is playing in the effort of their country, as well as of the political part they are called upon to play as citizens" (1942, 9).

Secondary and further education and youth services were meant to help each future citizen visualize his or her worth in the commonweal.

Political and educational analysts on the left and the right, including members of the Trade Unions Conference and the National Union of Conservative and Unionist Associations, criticized the report for its time delays and its perceived socialist (if not Communist) rhetoric. Critics on both sides of the aisle also suggested that the Conservative Sub-committee's reports were proto-Fascist and argued that it put England on the road toward, as *The Times* reported on October 26, 1942, "the nazification [*sic*] of young citizens." While other observers argued the report's errors were simply rhetorical, not philosophical, the criticism encouraged Butler to use caution in developing state-sponsored youth programs despite indications that Churchill approved of these plans in theory. Schemes for national educational trends such as youth services, that promoted a variety of further education and training while at the same time discouraging traditional biases about vocational training, meant progress in developing the bodies, minds, and spirits of professional and manual workers for the common good.

Along the line of spiritual development, the Sub-committee argued for a new state approach to religion, and crucially recommended in the 1942 "Educational Aims" that, "*Religion in the United Kingdom needs to be conceived, politically and administratively, in general terms as a basic and vital element in the national life, to be deliberately encouraged and fostered*" (26). The document contained a detailed analysis of the rights, responsibilities, and compromises that both the individual and the state would find necessary to create a system of religious and spiritual training that would best serve all interests (17-32). "Educational Aims" defined religion as a kind of "emotional awareness," through which "mankind seeks to comprehend its destiny," and which "is an essential condition of all social excellence" (1942, 25). This conception of Religious Education echoed Clarke's calls for the need for a philosophy in education.

The Sub-committee acknowledged that religion in England was an extremely difficult concept to pin down because of various views on religion and the state including religious differences and even "Agnosticism" ("Educational Aims" 1942, 18-25). The report's closing remarks on "the religious factor in education" nonetheless suggested that a "spiritual unity . . . must [be allowed] to grow, and grow by freedom no less than by direction" (38). The latter phrase acknowledged that religion in England was in flux. However, the summary conclusion of "Educational Aims" section on Religious Education stated:

> Every possible opportunity, encouragement, and assistance must be given by the State for the effective training of every child in the religious principles approved by its parents or guardian, provided that such training is not hostile to the State. Where such training is not available, the State must provide the most effective undenominational Christian teaching it can (1942, 38).

The Sub-committee was outspoken in proclaiming that its membership included Roman Catholics, Jews, Nonconformists, Anglicans, as well as "members . . . [who] would [not] claim active membership of any definite church or sect" ("Educational Aims" 1942, 17). They presented an argument and plan that first carefully weighed and discussed crucial issues involved in Religious Education and postwar Britain. Nonetheless, the Sub-committee's summary findings in "Educational Aims" clearly revealed that they believed the State's interests lay in ecumenical Christian education and training in the schools (38). They were not alone in these beliefs.

In November 1941, Lord Godfrey Elton, Oxford historian and Labour Party member, had published a controversial article in *The Daily Mail*. His piece boldly asked, "Are you a Christian?" and suggested that Britain's lack of promotion of Christian national culture in its educational system could affect the nation's overall strength on the world stage. Elton further argued: "It has been said that a nation that has once lost its faith is dying." In pointed rhetoric Elton's 1941 article asked, "Can we claim that Britain is Christian in anything approaching the sense in which Germany is Nazi?" He explained that Nazi philosophy was a central principle of the Nazi school system, entrenching Nazi thought into German society. He argued that Religious Education must become a natural and efficiently-taught part of the British system in order to counter the power of Nazi statism. He decried the religious vacuum he saw in state schools and accused the Board of Education and Butler of procrastination in implementing Religious Education effectively. Elton's article warned, "This war is a struggle for survival, after which the victor may shape the pattern of civilization for a thousand years. History knows no example of a civilization created by a people lacking a burning faith" (1941). For Elton, the break-down of effective national Religious Education had contributed to the desperate international situation England found itself in during World War II. Elton argued that the weakening of the Church and its schools and a perceived moral and religious vacuum within Britain were damaging the war effort and could lead to defeat, if not annihilation.

The Board of Education received Elton's message, in addition to other similarly dire predictions, and collected them in files including "Religious

Education in Schools—General" (1941). For example, Board official R. S. Wood noted in a letter dated October 22, 1941 that the British academic, Sir Walter Moberly, who also served as a collaborator on the *Christian News-Letter*, had stated that "the Church had entirely lost its grip on children." Therefore the government had a responsibility to step in to preserve the Christian character of the nation and its future citizens. Both statements bolstered coexisting calls for enforced Christian Religious Education in the schools. Butler, in fact, wrote to Elton on November 11, 1941 with a clarification of his personal feelings as well as the work the Board was undertaking in consultation with church officials. Butler's letter argued, "My heart is in this affair [surrounding Religious Education] but the Education Authorities and the Teachers must [also] be consulted." He was ready to move forward but knew he must use diplomacy and democratic methods to achieve reform. Fortuitously for Butler, increased ecumenical Christianity in the face of international threats was a popular rallying cry.

Because World War II created a unique sense of unity within England as a war fought by soldiers on the field but also by civilians at home, the whirlwind of the war efforts allowed a domestic settling of social and religious controversies. This sense of unity made Christian brother- and sisterhood, and more so English brother- and sisterhood, more important than any differences within the nation's cultural and social spheres, at least until the war's end. This spirit of unity was not just a popular sentiment, but had also smoothed over squabbles within and between political parties, allowing (if not demanding) the creation of a coalition government in England that produced such able negotiators as Butler, yet permitted the older-school politician Churchill to claim the prime ministership after his consistent anti-Nazi and pro-war stance since the early 1930s proved his foresight and mettle. War-time unity also enabled Christian sects, some of whom had been squabbling with each other for centuries, to see the war as more than England's stand against tyranny, but as English-Christianity's stand for "human civilization," engendered by their "Christian faith." A number of statements, including the latter, from *The Times*, February 13, 1941, were published as rallying cries for the general public. Once the battle against the "Godless," or at least, "Anti-Christian," forces had been secured, stated the aforementioned *Times* article, the nation could turn its attentions back to its own flock of lost sheep, children who were in danger of losing their connection with God, not to mention English-Christian religious culture. Religious and political leaders, now organized as the Christian Education Movement, issued a grave declaration of the situation facing Christian England during the war. In a 1942 joint statement,

"Christian Education," the Movement, including the Archbishops of Canterbury and York, and Members of Parliament, put a "choice before the Nation," asking,

> Is this New Order to be Christian, in the sense that those who plan it understand and accept the Christian view of man's nature and destiny . . . ? [T]o put it bluntly, do we or do we not care whether successive generations of children are taught to understand and accept the truth of God made known in Christ . . . ?

The combined threats of secularism, Communism, and Fascist statism compelled Christian sects in England to bury interdenominational disputes over Christian practice to protect Christianity itself as made clear in these public and political publications and special interest bulletins like the *Christian-Newsletter*.

The *Christian News-Letter* itself had been established in 1939 by J. H. Oldham in connection with the Council on the Christian Faith and the Common Life. Forty-eight collaborators were listed in the first issues including The Archbishop of York (William Temple), Fred Clarke, Canon F. A. Cockin, T. S. Eliot, Karl Mannheim, Walter Moberly, Walter Oakeshott, Dorothy Sayers, Arnold Toynbee, and R. H. Tawney. Oldham edited the *News-Letter* from 1939 to 1945 when editorship was taken over by Kathleen Bliss. Oldham began the *News-Letter* for two reasons, he argued in its first installment, "The first reason [for the *Christian News-Letter*] is that a grave situation calls for new concerted action. The present century has witnessed within what was once known as Christendom the vehement repudiation of the Christian tradition and a deliberate attempt to establish a post-Christian world." Oldham went on in this first installment to discuss the "disappoint[ment] and disillusion[ment]" of both Nazism and Communism and the disillusionment of youth. He and his collaborators hope that "an adventurous Christian faith [could] bring hope and renewal to a decaying civilization" through community collaboration and "bridg[ing] the gulf" between "organized religion and the general life of the community" (1939).

By 1942 Butler felt confident enough to begin making more direct public statements about Religious Education in the schools. In a speech to the National Union of Teachers (NUT), Butler argued, "Can we not . . . find some arrangement which, without doing violence to the conscience of the individual, gives recognition to the fact that ours is a Christian country by providing for the teaching of Christianity in all our schools?" (1942, 3). Similar statements by political, intellectual, and church leaders in the early

1940s made clear many in England were willing to work hard to form such an agreement.

Butler's 1942 speech to the NUT meticulously revealed an explicit call for Christian Religious Education in schools and the projects of educational civic humanism Butler had championed since 1938 and made pillars of his work at the Board of Education. Nonetheless, Butler had not forgotten Churchill's warning to avoid controversy. In his politic speech to the NUT he argued, "provided . . . we work together in a spirit of self-sacrifice and deny ourselves some of the undoubted satisfaction of pressing our own particular point of view . . . we may make progress together" (3). His first duty as a war-time reformer was to encourage consensus planning and agreement for the benefit of the nation. This philosophy was not political rhetoric but profound civic humanist ethics: Individual interests, at times, should be subdued for commonweal. Butler believed England could help extend these ethics beyond its own borders.

He spoke passionately to the NUT, for example, about the international consensus of the war: the "rising power of America, the massive staying power of Russia, [*sic*] and the historical resiliency of Britain and her Empire . . . sure to prevail over the clutching greed of . . . Japan, the prostrate and grasping Italy, and the false religion and false judgment of the Nazis" (1942, 2). This wartime international consensus complimented Butler's views on British power and community within the British Empire. An international feeling of community spirit provided Commonwealth countries (particularly Britain) with political and economic power, but Butler also believed that a Commonwealth relationship demanded duty and responsibility.[6] For Butler, the Commonwealth represented a practical, but democratically-based political and economic relationship: the British Empire was good for Britain, but working as a community of nations was good for all the Empire's citizens. This Commonwealth relationship paralleled his paradigm for domestic policy as well.

At a time when the English commonweal was confronting war and demographic decline, Butler believed government must extend its authority to compensate for the gaps left by laissez-faire policies. To support commonweal, officials and citizens must engage in "human planning," a point he made in his 1942 speech to the NUT. This meant the

[6] An earlier and clearer description of Butler's views on the British Empire, as a part of an important global network and a "Society of Nations," can be found in his address, "The Issues in British Foreign Policy," *International Affairs (Royal Institute of International Affairs 1931-1939)*, no. 3 May-June, 1938. *A National Faith*, especially chapters III–V and "The Future of Political Education" also reveal Butler's opinions about Britain's place in the world.

nation had to integrate its two, often conflicting, methods of education: liberal and vocational. Education and training should instead focus, specifically, on two points: individual students' interests and the needs of commonweal. Butler saw his vision of "human planning" as vitally different from the total statism of Nazis or the Communists: again, he argued to the NUT, "[we are] usually the most successful where we do not try to be too artificial, but leave something to chance and much to nature" (1942, 5). Statism and artificial social leveling were not beneficial, but evils that subdued the individual spirit, and thus in the long run did little to help fruitful national progress. Butler argued for broader, more general education, yet he also argued to the NUT, in connection to debates on secondary schools,

> We do not want the State education to become a racing stable out only to produce overtrained classic favorites. We *do* want to produce our racers, but also good healthy stock, frightened neither of the plough nor the shafts. As for our Bloodstock, I can only say that the less in-bred or "special" our leading strains in the educational world are, the better it will be for the future of the Nation (1942, 6).

The key here was Butler's belief in the need for what his colleague Mannheim would coin a "militant democracy:" planning for the future of the nation based on its current—and predicted—challenges: industrial, demographic, and imperial changes (1943). He outlined these plans in the body of his speech (1942, 3-7).

Along the lines of divisions of labor referred to symbolically as "racers," and "plough" horses, Butler discussed issues of "practical training" with the NUT which was a major theme of his work in reconstructing the educational system. In terms of types of education and training, Butler argued in his NUT speech, "This policy would not mean that every child should have the same education, or that we should do away with the diversity in our schools, or that absolute justice can be achieved." Rather, his speech argued, than "equality of opportunity" the educational system should rest on a "guiding principle" of "training suited to talents" in order to produce both the "plough" horses and "racers" that society needed to function. Butler suggested to the NUT that instead of an older ideal of a "career open to talents," "careers should be shut to those without talents." This did not mean that only those with talent in academics should get good jobs. Rather, in a time of demographic and economic uncertainty the idea of a good job would be reinterpreted to encompass all work that was necessary and beneficial to the nation. Parliamentary debates in both the Lords and the Commons in 1944 on

Butler's Education Bill reveal similar thinking was held by politicians on both sides of the aisle.

Instead of an academic meritocracy, meritocracy would be redefined to recognize a wider range of skills. Each student would be nurtured according to his or her individual merit and interests, whether practical, technical, or academic in nature. Butler argued against the potential waste maintained by training workers and professionals based on ideas of class and upward social mobility attached only to the professions. This waste *included* children from middle and upper class families whose aptitudes and interests were best suited for practical or industrial education rather than the professions their parents often choose for them along social, rather than commonweal, lines. Waste was also an issue when students from working class families, whose interests and aptitudes directed them to higher education and academic training, were denied these opportunities.

Butler supported practical education to encourage industrial growth and he supported workers as valuable and necessary to commonweal. The needs of industry, he argued, both in terms of economics and workers, should be carefully analyzed and weighed. Because the most practically-trained workers often supported the basic infrastructure of the nation, their education and happiness was integral to commonweal. As Butler told the NUT in 1942, "We must start early if we are to achieve the double purpose of helping the unskilled man to resist the numbing influence of the machine and of training the proportion of skilled men required to maintain our position as a leading industrial country" (6). Butler clearly believed that industry was the cornerstone of British civilization, but he was neither unaware, nor unsympathetic, to the socio-cultural difficulties associated with industrial labor and, more broadly, the working classes.

The crux of Butler's 1942 speech to the NUT proposed a "complete Reorganisation" of the educational system in practical terms. He argued, "I am opposed to nothing in the realm of the ideal . . . I am opposed to everything which promises the substance and which gives only the shadow" (4). He proceeded to outline for the NUT preliminary plans for educational reform with reference to his Board of Education Green Book report and opinions he had gathered "going round the country." The 1942 speech to the NUT made references to a number of Board of Education investigations underway into examinations, industry, "the training and supply of teachers and youth leaders," as well as questions that must be raised in regard to the health and further education of youth, training colleges, and spreading and deepening knowledge of both the United States of American and "Russia." This meant, Butler told the NUT, "We should take care to choose, and then train for positions of responsibility in whatever sphere they may be called to serve, the very best out of our richly-stocked young material" (5). As important as these goals were, however, Butler made clear to the NUT that first and foremost was that the nation exit the war "as one single society" (5). For Butler, this meant healing divisions in educational communities including those among religious sects and between secular and Religious Education.

In reference to the dual system and Religious Education, Butler spoke clearly to the NUT about an agreement to be reached between [secular] education and "the Churches:" the need for "elevating to a proper status ethical standards and the moral character of our national personality" (1942, 3 and 7). While he alluded to the deep conflicts between the churches, as well as individual belief systems, he argued for an ecumenical Christian conviction within the school system. He told the NUT, "Revolutions exploit another part of human nature hitherto neglected" and argued that the nation must shore up its culture and spirit: "the soul of men" (7). This soul must be nurtured from a young age to lay down solid foundations for social harmony.

To help build these foundations in England, in 1942 Butler appointed a Youth Advisory Council to consider the position of a comprehensive youth service; the resulting "The Youth Service after the War" report was published in 1943. This document made special references to young people between ages fourteen and eighteen as a loose definition of youth past compulsory school-age, yet not fully adults (5). Within this age group the Council's focus was on those young people "whose gifts and interests are not academic" (7). This was not meant to limit or classify these students but to offer specialized education and training to students who might not enter formal higher education. The Council noted in its report that these judgments were based on contemporary educational research that argued, "the majority of young people do not find satisfaction in an academic atmosphere even during school years and school hours" (10). Thus, service to non-academically-minded youth would include finding ways to better engage them in life-long learning, training, cultural activities, and recreation.

The Youth Advisory Council's report emphasized the vital connections between home and school, work and leisure, as well as the influence of religion in lives of young people. It also argued that in relation to civic education, stronger connections needed to be made between the "duties and responsibilities" and the "rights and benefits" of "a sound civilization" (6). In relation to this argument, the Council admitted that, "[English] education has in the past undoubtedly been biased towards the academic rather than the practical, the manual or the domestic" (10). Emphasizing a reconciliation of modern industrialism and capitalism with a united community spirit, the Council argued,

> The remedy for [more monotonous professions] is not to draw social distinctions between one kind of employment and another but to make all workers everywhere realize the inspiring truth that their work, whatever it is, is an essential contribution to the life and well-being of the community (10).

In this way duties and responsibilities could be reconciled with rights and benefits to maintain an evolution, rather than cyclical social antagonisms leading to potential revolution.

In its 1943 report, the Youth Advisory Council also stressed the need for increasing the rights and benefits of disenfranchised youth by raising the school-leaving age and increasing the variety of educational and recreational activities to improve youth morale (5-14). The Council's clearest statement of liberty tempered by duty was philosophical rather than bureaucratic: "An activity voluntarily undertaken may involve submission to authority, instruction, discipline, and even command, but being voluntarily undertaken, could form an important part of leisure" (12). This suggested that service to one's country, if performed willingly with a spirit of civic pride, could transcend the dangerous example of Nazism which loomed over Europe. In order to achieve these goals, the Council stressed coordination among local further education, youth services, and voluntary associations, as well as among state, local, and voluntary agencies. For example, the Council's report recommended the integration of youth into local and national communities through leisure activities designed to help youth grow into adult life rather than "keep them back unduly in the atmosphere and surroundings of adolescence" (15). An underlying message to these agencies was that youth guidance was best achieved with a mixture of formal and informal methods of a broadly-conceived education including liberal arts, but also vocational training, recreation for health and fitness, and organized and free-play leisure activities.

Sharp criticism launched at plans for compulsory youth service as well as the resistance of the Ministry of Labour and the Home Office to working closely with Education, however, engendered a shift from nationally-driven youth services to youth services embedded in local schemes for further education and voluntary associations. The Board of Education continued to plan and work with local and national agencies to promote youth service within schemes of further education as were laid out in the 1943 report "The Youth Service after the War." Rhetoric describing youth services, however, softened from the more fervent demands of "A Plan for Youth," to calls for expanded further education that would emphasize individual and community needs. Contemporary analysis of public anxieties signaled that community needs included enriching the nation's spiritual life.

The advent of the war and fears of the spread of revolutionary politics had encouraged Christian leaders to embrace Christian ecumenical values to support a civil society. Christian leaders and educationalists continued to suggest education as the medium for renewed ecumenical religious instruction. The spread of fascism and communism, for example, had led the Archbishop of Canterbury, William Temple, to state fears in his July 14, 1943 *Times* article, "A Duty to Youth," that youth denied their "fellowship" with God would become "a fertile seed plot for revolutionary ideas which usually had little enough about them of faith in God or charity towards men." In Temple's mind, educational reform and religious instruction in schools were necessary both to boost national spirit and to protect the nation from the secular, revolutionary ideologies that threatened to invade England. The deepening crises of the war catalyzed this official effort and encouraged even secular-minded private citizens to rethink their religious faith. A young secretary and professed agnostic summed up this frame of mind, explaining, "Since the war began [I] have often felt I wished I could believe in a God. The suffering the war causes is so great that one wants . . . help of a spiritual kind" (Mass-Observation 1943). Religious and professed agnostic citizens returned to Christian ethics as an anchor in the war's chaotic culture.

By request of the *Christian News-Letter,* Mass-Observation investigated and reported on the mindset of the war-time public in relation to religion. Their 1943 report, "Religion and the People," concluded: "There is widespread *desire* for religion to take a bigger part in the life of the community, a common goodwill and tolerance towards religious faith and inspiration, which needs (and often consciously wants) some definite sign that organized religion is in fact determined to play a better and more active part in social life." This report was nuanced, but gave assurance to politicians and educationalists interested in renewing Religious Education's spirit that they had their fingers on the pulse of the nation. For example, the 1943 Mass-Observation report made heartening points about "religious alignments to-day." The first could be read as negative but contained a positive statement about the social importance of the soft power of religion: "It is difficult to obtain accurate data on the strength and importance of personal religious beliefs, because it is the socially done thing to say one has a religious faith, however dim and meaningless that faith may be." This type of statement could be offered as evidence of secularization, but it also spoke to the lasting socio-cultural, if not sacred, importance of religion and Christianity in England. It suggested that while sacred faith was a difficult concept to concretely define, English citizens held to a faith of Christian ethics or traditions as part of their national identity.

Although the Mass-Observation report did corroborate officials' fears that many English were moving away from organized or institutionalized church-based religion, and were especially skeptical of official religion as proffered by the churches, it also revealed that not all hope was lost. Skepticism about organized religion was on the rise but the war suggested to Christians and secularists that spiritual, or at least moral, faith was still necessary for civilized society. In response to their publication of Mass-Observation's 1943 report, the *Christian News-Letter's* February 10, 1943 edition argued "Action—or practical, simply-understood and unambiguous tokens of forthcoming action—might quickly transform widespread passive goodwill into something dynamic, in the religious as in the political sphere." Christian intellectuals were eager to provide guidance in faith and philosophy to help fill the public desire for a renewed sense of spirituality and faith. Much could be achieved through Christian education. Christians continued to press for Religious Education as part of educational reconstruction. Their hopes for reformed Religious Education were soon publically confirmed by none other than Prime Minister Churchill—much to the delight of Butler.

CHAPTER FIVE

FOR GOD AND COUNTRY

> Hammered on the anvil of this war, our nation has been shaped to a new unity of pride and purpose . . . as the [Education] reforms are made effective . . . we shall develop our most abiding assets and richest resources—the character and competence of a great people.
> —R. A. Butler, Parliamentary Debates, (Commons), January 19, 1944

If Prime Minister Winston Churchill had truly expected R. A. Butler to follow his orders to remain passive on issues of educational reconstruction he had sorely misjudged his new President of the Board of Education. Butler had quietly gone about the business of postwar educational reconstruction including addressing the religious conflicts. In 1943, Churchill was finally able to turn his attention from military issues to postwar domestic issues, including education, because victory seemed close at hand. By 1943 Butler and his colleagues—fortuitously it turned out—had already laid much of the groundwork for the Education Bill they would submit. Indeed, Butler recounts in his memoir that on the night of March 11, 1943, during a weekend retreat at Chequers, Churchill asked Butler to read and revise a speech on postwar reconstruction he was planning to present to the nation. He indicated he would interrogate Butler on the speech's remarks on education the next morning.

Butler read the speech and feverishly expanded and edited Churchill's remarks on educational reconstruction and reform. He recalled his late-night editing session:

> I sat up for a considerable period rewriting [the sections on education.] In particular, I added a piece on religion and its place in the schools, modified the reference to the school-leaving age by saying that it must be progressively prolonged, inserted a few lines on further education and part-time release from industry . . . and substituted for the rather rude remarks about the old school tie a statement about the need for every type of school and every type of tie (1971, 114).

Butler's revisions revealed to Churchill Butler's behind-the-scenes work on educational reconstruction. Butler also recalls in his memoir confessing to Churchill that weekend: "With the aid of my colleagues . . . 'I am drafting an Education Bill'" (1971, 115). Luckily for Butler, by this time Churchill had relaxed his adamant refusal to consider educational reforms, and his response to Butler's confession was subdued yet responsive. Butler recalls Churchill confiding in him that he had already promised his daughter to include a remark in his upcoming speech on an earlier (vaguely defined) promise to increase the school-leaving age to sixteen (1971, 115). Butler's revisions to Churchill's speech helped clarify educational reform proposals the Board of Education had already begun to develop.

Ten days later Churchill broadcast the speech live to the war-torn nation, and *The Times* reprinted the speech the following morning, March 22, under the headline "Four Years' Plan for Britain." In the speech Churchill outlined the basic tenets of Butler's forth-coming bill for educational reconstruction. The speech also served as an official public announcement of the educational reform plans Butler had been orchestrating since before his appointment to the Board of Education. Churchill emphasized the national characteristics that had both allowed the nation to persevere against the Nazis, and would allow the country to rebuild after the war. These qualities, Churchill noted, included Christian faith and values. In fact, assisted by the ideas and proposals of Butler, Churchill's speech gave special emphasis to religion's "fundamental" place in English life and its educational system (March 22, 1943.) In this speech, Churchill called the Christian religion, "a rock in the life and the character of the British people," and an "element which should never be banished from our system of education." Butler notes that he arranged to "vet" the speech before its delivery to ensure it did not interfere with or contradict his plans for an Education Bill, and that after the speech he received "a brief acknowledgment from No. 10: 'Thank you so much for your help [with the speech]'" (1971, 116). With Churchill's speech to the nation, Butler had symbolically crossed the crest of Pisgah and could continue his path to the Promised Land with plans for an Education Bill in hand.

Only months later, in July 1943, Butler was able to introduce his White Paper, "Educational Reconstruction," to Parliament. Butler prepared this policy paper to continue and engender more discussion, rather than moving straight for a bill, as a diplomatic move to ensure the forthcoming bill would meet with as little resistance as possible. "Educational Reconstruction" reiterated earlier proposals, such as the 1938 Spens report, following educational policy trends of the time. It also emphasized philosophical considerations including the freedom and responsibilities local authorities and individual schools would need to make a secondary multilateral system work. Butler's White Paper, "Educational Reconstruction," noted that these philosophical considerations came with a practical caveat: local educational authorities would have to adhere to necessary limits of "convenience and efficiency" in school organization (10). The White Paper argued, however, "It would be wrong to suppose that [grammar, modern, and technical] schools will necessarily remain separate and apart" (10).

The White Paper's emphasis was the need for a variety of types of students and future citizens to benefit the national well-being, not rigid tripartism in the educational system. Rather, the White Paper emphasized, as long as efficient and convenient, school organizations could include "the free interchange of pupils from one type of education to another" (10). It also emphasized the personal responsibilities parents and teachers must take in helping students choose a school and field of study. Thus "Educational Reconstruction" argued against reliance on standardized placement examinations—the British term is the eleven plus—for secondary school assignments. Rather, Butler's White Paper suggested, "children at about the age of 11 should be classified, not on the results of a competitive test, but on an assessment of their individual aptitudes largely by such means as school records, supplemented, if necessary, by intelligence tests, due regard being had to their parents' wishes and the careers they have in mind" (9). These tenets followed recommendations that had also been made by the 1941 Consultative Committee's Norwood report.

In terms of Religious Education, "Educational Reconstruction" argued that a variety of educationalists had confirmed a "general wish" for Religious Education to be given "a more defined place in the life and work of the schools, springing from the desire to revive the spiritual and personal values of . . . society" (1943, 11). The White Paper suggested that every school day should thus begin with a "corporate act of worship," that religious instruction should be structured by an agreed-upon syllabus designed by the Anglican and Non-conformist churches, teachers and the local authority, and that limitations on Religious Education should be removed from school schedules (11-12). These suggestions did, however, maintain the precedent of the 1870 Cowper-Temple clause. In spirit and form, Butler's White Paper, "Educational Reconstruction," through emphases on secondary and Religious Education, encompassed Christian-civic humanism in reformed education.

Butler and his colleagues had envisioned an educational system that catered to the nation's economic and social needs, not just its academic educational traditions. Their proposed legislation included suggestions for a variety of what were seen as practical education programs and youth services to achieve these goals. This included proposals for youth services and further education developed by the McNair Committee, appointed in 1942—a group which included Fred Clarke. This work helped mend what Clarke and others had noted was an unfortunate division between cultural and vocational life. In terms of economics, the reformed educational system would allow the training of a broad range of students to work in the diverse array of vocations necessary for a modern, industrialized democracy. Secondary and higher education combined with youth services and further education were planned to fill these needs. Socio-economically diverse educational and training opportunities would be balanced with an increased spirit of patriotism and Christian brother- and sisterhood engendered by Religious Education. By bridging cultural-vocational educational divides, reaffirming Christian-civic ethics, and allowing the nation's industrial, professional, and intellectual bases to grow practically and efficiently, "Educational Reconstruction" could help the nation traverse the postwar era.

Educational philosophy aside, political realities were of concern as well. Constructing a successful Education Bill rested in large part on Butler's handling of the church-state dual system and practical politics. In order to secure educational reform, Butler had to solve three interrelated problems: He must placate and ensure peace between Christian sects, create a feasible solution to the financial woes of church schools, and balance the economics of national education. Although the church schools faced financial problems which left them unable to meet modern curriculum trends, Butler needed to compromise with church leaders to maintain the dual system after the war. This was an expedient economic move, as the churches, particularly the Church of England, still served a vast number of students across the country. In addition, the Church possessed enough political power to disrupt, if not destroy, Butler's plans for educational reform. Butler knew he was facing hardline religious activists in his educational reform plans and he realized that the religious settlement was not, in the words of historian of education Michael Barber, ". . . an *alternative* to an educational reform which would have improved . . . education, it was a *precondition* to it" (1994, 119). Butler did face political and economic pressure to continue the dual system, yet these demands fail to adequately explain why the state *mandate* of Religious Education was proposed in a nation with already entrenched Religious

Education. Political and economic answers also fail to explain how a Religious Education mandate in a supposedly secularizing nation engendered minimal protest. Answers may be found, however, in war-time and postwar responses to religious life and spiritualism.

F. E. Moreton, author of a 1944 article, "Attitudes to Religion," provided a cultural explanation of the support for the mandate of Religious Education and instruction in the schools. Moreton's analysis, based on Mass-Observation data and educational proposals conducted in the early 1940s, confirmed earlier analysis of the separation between the general public and the churches. Moreton noted, however, that public sentiment toward religion was much more favorable than public sentiment toward the institutions of the churches. In addition, Moreton found that public sentiment toward Religious Education in schools was also positive. In general, he found a public desire, if not demand, for religious teaching in the schools. These kinds of reports, in addition to clergy's and intellectual's promotion of Christian ecumenicalism, indicated that Religious Education in the schools had the general support of the people. The public believed that Christian-based Religious Education could provide to students the moral philosophy the country was desperately seeking. The spirit of war-time ecumenicalism and public sentiment for increased Religious Education allowed Butler and his colleagues to negotiate successfully proposals for not just expecting, but *requiring*, Religious Education across the dual system. This consensus allowed politicians and educationalists to spend the bulk of their energy on proposals for expanding secular educational concerns, with Religious Education largely an accepted part of the forthcoming Act.

In response to "Educational Reconstruction," the highly respected H. C. Dent, editor of the *Times Educational Supplement*, applauded the White Paper for "mak[ing] possible the greatest and grandest educational advance this country has ever known" (1943, 7). Nonetheless, he argued it held "outstanding defects" in "the almost unbelievable leisureliness of the stages by which it is to reach fruition, and the meager expenditure on which it is expected to happen" (1943, 17 and 7). As an educationalist, Dent wanted rapid progress. As a wartime politician, Butler was limited in expediency as well as the grandeur of his planning. Nevertheless, he successfully sent a landmark Education Bill to Parliament only three years after taking office, despite the difficult challenges of the war and the difficult climate of English educational and practical politics. The "Educational Reconstruction" bill received its first Parliamentary reading in December, 1943. The Bill engendered passionate speeches and some debate within both Houses. Nonetheless, its passage through Parliament was relatively quick and painless.

Given the precarious state of English finances and society in 1944, both Houses of Parliament engaged in discussion of the Education Bill between January and June 1944 with eyes wide-open to myriad political and social issues. These ranged from what educational reform meant on domestic and international fronts, including Fascist threats to the educational system, to practical concerns over the need for teachers, buildings, books, and necessary financial arrangements. On April 5, 1944, Parliamentary Secretary Chuter Ede made a speech in the House of Commons pertaining specifically to educational and financial matters. In August of the same year, The Earl of Selborne, Minister of Economic Welfare (aka Lord Wolmer), made a speech in the Lords, which was subsequently reprinted in *The Times* as "Religious Teaching in Schools: Suggested Safeguards for New Schemes," in which he argued,

> The President of the Board of Education proposed a complete reconstruction of our educational system, and a wide extension of it in many directions. The fulfillment of the scheme c[an] not be achieved for a number of years. Hundreds of new schools would have to be built, thousands of schools would need to be structurally improved, and tens of thousands of teachers would have to be recruited and trained. There [is] also the financial aspect to be considered (August 5, 1944).

Yet Parliamentary discussions of practical educational infrastructures and their necessary funding were tempered by fervent speeches on philosophical issues of reforming educational systems including social justice and religious faith. Members of Parliament, too, worked as "devotees at the shrine of [educational] progress."

In the Commons, for example, Sir Arnold Grimley argued on February 9, 1944, "We have to raise the status of the fellow who works in overalls higher than that of the man who wears a black coat and a white collar and sits in an office." These were not comments made in support of radical socialist revolutions, but arguments developed within the historical context of the 1940s to maintain and reinvigorate England's agricultural and industrial-capitalist bases, its citizenry, and its community spirit. Once again, educational waste referred to middle and upper-middle class youths who were wasting time and energy pursuing goals of professional and academic education for upward social mobility without consideration for their individual aptitudes or the more practical economic needs of the nation. Educational waste was not just an issue surrounding working-class students denied higher and further education.

Between February and June 1944 members of the Commons such as Earl Winterton and Sir George Schuster spoke of increasing vocational education in terms of technical, scientific, and agricultural education. In the Lords, the Earl of Selborne, supported by Lord Roche, argued that "one of the great failures of our education system in the past has been that it has turned out not only too many black-coated workers, but also men and especially women who are quite uneducated in those fundamentally important subjects [technology, domestic science, and agriculture]."

Mr. Woodburn in the Commons supported this line of thought, arguing on February 9, "The great majority of the people of this country want their children trained in order to get a good position in society . . . [Yet] [p]eople are not being educated for the life that they are going to live; 95 per cent. are being educated for the life they are not going to live. Education must have some connection with life." So while state-mandated "equality" in education continued to be rejected as an English educational philosophy because, as Gary McCulloch reports, "[it] smack[ed] too much of Bolshevism," members of both Houses realized the need to bridge the cultural-vocation divide (1994, 85-87). Contemporary political trends precluded radical forms of egalitarianism. Progressive social trends, however, would allow a reassessment of what constituted social success.

Nonetheless, Members of Parliament viewed educational reconstruction as a cultural as well as socio-economic challenge. Lord Latham argued in the Lords on June 8 that "the cultural aspect of education must be emphasized, those elements in education which . . . teach the young not necessarily how to make a living, but how to live." In the Commons, Captain Cobb had stated in February a similar concern: "it would be an evil thing for the boys and girls of this country if technical education was made a hard and fast thing and no other education was envisaged." Parliamentary Secretary of Education Chuter Ede, however, offered an explanation for stagnation in English education tied to social problems and cultural ideals:

> [W]e have somewhat inadequately kept the motto 'Manners maketh the man,' by making it appear that correct manners means the wearing of a black coat and pinstripe trousers. Why do parents desire that their children shall get into secondary schools of the [grammar] type? It is because they are the avenue to . . . the 'safety-first' jobs . . . One cannot blame the parents in our industrial populations . . . for saying, 'Well, if my boy or girl has any choice, it shall not be industry, but the office for them' . . . industry [positions are] regarded as being much lower in status than the others (February 8, 1944).

Chuter Ede's argument stressed that cultural values tied to ideals of individual social status, rather than practical issues for the public good, distorted English ideas about what a good education was and where it was acquired. Ede's comments also pin-pointed some problems in formal academic education: training students in the mechanics of professionalization for "'safety-first' jobs" made the academic work of the grammar school little more than technical training for "the office." It did not fulfill elements of liberal education and training that could lead to future happiness, and the social role it filled did not provide the nation with energetic or inventive intellectuals or workers.

At the same time, the possibility was open that some students could find self-worth and fulfillment in manual work either through personal fulfillment or through service to the national community. The importance of this work, Sir Harold Webbe added in the February 8 Commons debate, was obvious:

> It ought not to be necessary to argue the importance of technical education. We are a great industrial nation which [must] grow all the food it can and . . . pay [for imported food] by the products of its industries. It is obvious that the standard of living of our people, indeed our continued existence as a great Power, depends fundamentally on the maintenance of our agriculture and industry.

Similar sentiments appeared in debates in the House of Lords between February and June 1944: Lord Roche argued in Parliament in support of increased agricultural and technical education, "The countryside is strewn with the products of the secondary schools, little shopgirls and clerks who ought to be in something much more useful and better" (July 11).

If this was snobbery and bias, it was directed at the wasted potential of students being trained for menial middle-class work, rather than educated for modern agriculture and technology—areas of the economy Roche believed needed a boost. Members of Parliament argued that both kinds of education, vocational and academic, if properly reformed, could prepare students for a place in the social, economic, and cultural sphere.

Butler had himself summed up the crux of these debates early on, in a speech to Commons on January 19, 1944. In regard to citizenship and the transcendence of a cultural-vocational and socio-vocational divide, Butler argued,

> We hope to institute the broader training of a citizen for all . . . I think it is time to say that education should be the ally and not the dreaded competitor of employment. To the question 'Who will do the work if

> everybody is educated?' we reply that education itself will oil the wheels of industry and will bring a new efficiency, the fruit of modern knowledge, to aid the ancient skill of farm and field . . . In the new attitude to secondary education we have two main objectives. The first is that, as far as possible, provision of various types of education should be accessible to all, whatever their social or financial circumstances; and secondly, that traditions and standards which have been a feature of our British education should, so far as possible, be preserved. There is no desire to 'level down'; there is only a desire to bring everybody, ever upward.

In his January 19 speech to Parliament, Butler also discussed the meaning behind religious instruction as written in the Bill and discussed by Parliament, arguing, "Let us hope that our children seek for themselves in Christianity principles which give a purpose to life and a guide to all its problems." Members of Parliament came to agree on the need for a reestablishment of Christianity and Christian ethics at the base of society by requiring students to learn and worship the Gospel at school. Lord Wolmer had disclosed this movement's philosophy in his 1941 statement "Christian Education," which was brought to Butler's personal attention: "The war . . . revealed to us the need for a national re-consideration of the whole problem of the moulding of the character of our future citizens in face of the difficult days which lie ahead." By the time the Board of Education had presented the Education Bill to Parliament, members of both Houses had come to understand the need for mandatory Religious Education in both political and cultural terms. For example, on June 6, 1944 Lord Quickswood made more specific Wolmer's fears:

> We must face the fact that we live in a time of great religious crisis. The movement which has been so desolating Germany and Italy will certainly spread all over the world; indeed it has, in one form or another, spread everywhere. There is a widespread tendency to substitute the worship of man for the worship of God.

Even more clearly, however, Members of Parliament believed that England was a Christian nation and that the state school system should reflect this national culture and belief system. As Members of Parliament had argued in their 1942 "Why Christian Education Matters," "The struggle in which we are engaged is clearly one [against] a regime embracing a crude and reactionary paganism, finding expression in material force." Their solution: "the declared purpose of establishing ['the Christian philosophy of life'] more firmly in the common life of the World as the foundation of . . . [a] new and better social order." They suggested Religious Education in English schools to help the nation embrace, as

Butler had argued, values guided by something other than materialism. Members of Parliament such as Lord Nathan maintained this line of reasoning in 1944 Parliamentary deliberations in the Lords. Nathan argued,

> Politics and economics are means only, and not ends; they have to have their ends set for them by moral law, and in our European civilization it is the ideas embodied in the Christian ethic which can alone supply that moral law. It is right, therefore, that the system of British education . . . should be given full recognition to that fact and effective application to that principle.

In England Religious Education had long been defined as instruction associated with one of the two main Christian denominations—Anglican and Non-conformist—already within England and this definition had not yet shifted toward serious concerns for religious pluralism beyond some nods to Catholicism and Judaism. Members of Parliament debating the language of the bill clearly held to the narrower Christian definition of "denomination," and Religious Education as Protestantism.

The threats and contradictions of a more loosely defined statement on Religious Education in twentieth-century England were not completely lost on Members of Parliament. This hardened calls for specific language to make it clear that Religious Education meant Christianity—and Protestant thinking at that. In the House of Commons, MP H. Brooke and others argued on March 10, 1944 that the word "Christian" should be specifically added to the Bill: "It would then be clear beyond all doubt that Parliament intended the act of worship and religious instruction in schools to be in accordance with the views of the Christian Churches of this country." In the House of Lords, The Lord Archbishop of Canterbury, William Temple, agreed, arguing on June 6, 1944,

> I have been much exercised by the question whether it is sufficient to speak of religious instruction or whether we ought not to aim at speaking of Christian instruction . . . The prospect of giving instruction in the tenets of Islam, Hinduism, Buddhism, Shintoism, Taoism and others to children under fifteen, leaving them afterwards to form a judgment upon their merits, is rather alarming with anyone familiar with the practice of teaching.

Temple was not overly concerned with the language, however, concluding this statement with, "There is no doubt, I think, what is the intention of the Government."

This point was made even clearer in the House of Lords several weeks later, on June 21, when The Lord Bishop of Chichester, George Kennedy Allen Bell, once again raised the question by stipulating more directly that religious instruction was to be Christian in nature. Bell argued, "I do believe that, in these extremely uncertain times, if religious instruction is to be made compulsory the faith in which instruction is to be given should be specified." He was persuaded to drop, or at least seriously reconsider his position, after the Earl of Selborne, Lord Wolmer, pointed out during the June 21 debate an earlier argument that both the government and Parliament were firmly agreed that both religious instruction and worship in schools should be Christian. Furthermore, Wolmer argued that, "if we put in an Act of Parliament that a syllabus has to be in accordance with the Christian faith, it is open to any one of His Majesty's subjects to bring before the secular courts of this country the question of whether a particular syllabus is in accordance with the Christian faith or not." This, he pointed out, could open up whole new episodes of "trouble" akin to the denominational disagreements of the nineteenth centuries. Thus, for 1940s England, Religious Education would be synonymous with, but not legislated as, Christian education.

In the end, politicians did not formally designate Religious Education as Christian. There is no doubt, however, that the government and Parliament were in agreement about Religious Education's explicit meaning (dominantly Protestant Christianity) but needed to avoid conflict or partisan wrangling.[7] Furthermore, both Churchill's and Butler's comments on the issue shored up confidence in the Board of Education's plans for a Christian religious instruction. In an address to the House of Lords on June 7, for example, Butler argued for the "hope that our children may gain knowledge of the common Christian faith held by their fathers for nearly 2,000 years." His math was fuzzy, but Butler's words indicated a historical memory in England that tied to contemporary life what many saw as the glorious beginning of English history in Christianity and the Roman Empire. Christianity, Butler and his colleagues hoped, could continue to serve as a guiding light and cohesive commonality between English citizens.

The goals of Parliament, then, paralleled the Christian-civic humanism described by Butler, Clarke, Mannheim and their colleagues: an educational system that addressed philosophical and practical concerns. The goals were to maintain necessary economic diversity while uniting the nation

---

[7] Archival evidence reveals limited protest against this Religious Education settlement by Roman Catholics, Jews, and secular thinkers. See for examples, "Religious Education in Schools," (1941) and "Rationalists Take a Hand" (1941).

and its people with a common spiritual and moral connection. National unity did not necessitate social uniformity. In his January 19 speech to Commons Butler argued,

> An educational system by itself, cannot fashion the whole future structure of a country, but it can make better citizens. Plato said, 'The principle which our laws have in view is to make the citizens as happy and harmonious as possible.' Such is the modest aim of this Bill which provides a new framework for promoting the natural growth and development not only of children, but of national policy itself towards education in the years to come. . . [I]nstead of 'the rudiments of letters,' we offer [the 'spiritual, moral, mental, and physical development of the community'] and onwards an opportunity to every child.

Butler found Parliament in tune with this philosophy, and the Education Bill passed into law little more than a year after Churchill's speech "Four Years' Plan for Britain," with Royal Assent on August 3, 1944. It carried the blessings of Churchill, Parliament, the Protestant churches, the general public and a wide-range of educationalists—including for example, H. C. Dent, Helen C. Cole, and Shena Simon. All celebrated the passing of this "landmark in education" with praise and largely constructive criticism on general and specific directives of the Act.

The 1944 Education Act, then and now, was particularly significant for several reasons: It worked to push forward over-due reform that included extending the school leaving age and expanding the secondary school system; and it promised increased social democracy within education but aimed its efforts at the educational needs of the country and the social reality of the times. It was part and parcel of state welfare reforms that would evolve into the Welfare State. The 1944 Act was a historic piece of state welfare legislation aimed to pull England from the mire of domestic and international turmoil that had so plagued its people during the first half of the twentieth century and push it forward economically, socially, and culturally into the postwar era. In addition to its role in the creation of schemes of secondary education for all, the Act enacted important legislation for mandatory part-time further education and county colleges. Last, but certainly not least, it mandated Religious Education in the educational system. For all its initial successes, however, the implementation of sections of the Act would be fraught with difficulties.

The Act's legacy would be first and foremost evaluated by its role in the economy and society of the postwar decades rather than by its intentions. For all its relatively smooth construction and passage, and its lauded initial successes, implementation of key practical-minded sections of the Act would be fraught with difficulties and some, such as schemes for further education, never fully coalesced. The Act's cultural legacy, too, was misunderstood as England, like much of the Western world, seemed to secularize. Religious Education, however, turned out to play a more vital role than once thought as many English citizens tried to reclaim their traditional Christian character—at least rhetorically—in the early twenty-first century. With the benefit of hindsight, twenty-first century historians would do well to remember that the architects of the Act built their legislation on *Christian*-civic tenets. While provisions for secondary education for all have been lauded as *the* landmark in education in 1944 Chapters 6 and 7 examine how Christian-civic humanism, through Religious Education and secondary and further education and youth services, was imagined as the groundwork of the Act.

CHAPTER SIX

RELIGIOUS EDUCATION FOR ALL

> Perhaps on the long view the best work we did in 1944 was to enshrine for the future in English educational law the ancient and unalterable truth that the fear of the Lord is the beginning of knowledge.
> —R. A. Butler, "The 1944 Act Seen against the Pattern of the Times," 1952

Political and cultural anxieties during the war years had prevented Butler and his coalition colleagues from making bold policy statements that might be misinterpreted as radical politics. As a result, the language of the 1944 Education Act was less explicit than recommendations such as those made by the Conservative Sub-committee on Education. Bipartisan criticism of the Sub-committee's reports had suggested to prudent politicians that the 1944 Act's language be tempered for public and Parliamentary consumption. In addition, Butler and his colleagues understood—and argued in documents such as "The Future of Political Education" (Butler 1939)—that in the postwar world educational and social systems would require flexibility to withstand the flux of rapid global change. Flexibility would better allow England and the British Commonwealth to maintain their historic place as an economic, cultural, and political powerhouse. Thus, as Butler himself noted in the Commons on January 19, 1944, the Act was written as a philosophical guide for future administrators rather than set-in-stone educational policy. The 1944 Act served as a framework for reconnecting the nation's cultural and economic traditions, as well as using education to reconnect citizens to a vision of an organic, democratic, commonweal. The Act's legislation, however, was not always rigidly precise about the paths to these goals, because it promoted social reform for state welfare rather than a statist social revolution.

In addition to this politic rhetoric key sections of the Act, including those implementing secondary, religious, and further education, were postponed until April 1945 so that essential infrastructure could be put into place before carrying out the Act's guidelines. This meant in practice that the architects of the Act's educational policies and philosophy were not necessarily its construction workers. Butler's Board of Education shifted to a Labour-controlled Ministry of Education by May 1945. As a result, Butler left Education in 1945. Thus, postwar political transitions, including shifts in educational philosophies and priorities combined with years of postwar austerity, contributed to sometimes wooly interpretations of the Act's main educational and structural tenets.

Nonetheless, however the Act was eventually implemented, the Act's political and intellectual architects designed its principles to promote Christian-civic humanism through religious, secondary, and further education in schools. Sections 7 and 8, 25-30, 41-47 and supplementary materials set out those reformist educational policy decisions. In addition to the language of the Act itself, discussions and analysis surrounding the Act's legislation as well as supplementary religious educational materials including textbooks and syllabi reveal the Act, in its specific historical context, set out commonly understood and acceptable goals as guiding principles of the Act. This literature also reveals that the Act's role as "a landmark in education" went beyond its historic reorganization of elementary and secondary education into a plan for lifelong learning for all, to include a progressive educational philosophy promoting "spiritual, moral, mental, and physical development of the community" as stated in section 7 of the 1944 Act. These goals were consonant with Christian-civic humanism in education.

The 1944 Act, in structure and philosophy, reflected the spirit of pre-Labour state welfare ideals. It clearly stipulated a myriad of social services related to health, nourishment, and clothing which local educational authorities (LEAs) must provide as part of an integrated social welfare system. The Act comprised 122 sections that included broad social welfare measures such as specific provisions for milk and meals for students by each LEA. The Act also provided for key administrative shifts such as the aforementioned establishment of a Ministry, rather than Board, of Education. The development of the Ministry was significant in state welfare because it symbolized a centralization of English education while at the same time allowing LEAs to maintain control of issues related to regional education. The Act stipulated that separate elementary, secondary, and further education systems be provided for all students, rather than the system of elementary education for many, secondary and higher education for few. The architects of the Act, however, suggested secondary schools be provided to cater to students', parents', and local authorities' desires and needs under a system of separate but equal facilities. These facilities could include grammar schools, technical schools, modern schools, or a mix of types under bipartite and tripartite systems. This served goals of state welfare on individual, local, and national levels.

The Act restructured the basic educational system in section 7, "The Three Stages of the System," and section 8, which stated the "duty of local education authorities to secure provision of primary and secondary schools" (4-5). These sections have long been interpreted as simply structural in nature. They were, however, underscored with a Christian-civic educational philosophy. Section 7 is worth repeating: "It shall be the duty of the local education authority for every area . . . to contribute towards the *spiritual, moral, mental, and physical development* of the community by securing that efficient education . . . be available to meet the needs of the population of their area [emphasis added]" (4). This statement stressed an educational philosophy for commonweal, rather than the politics of individual school or student identity.

Sections 7 and 8, however, were only two of the landmark statements or policies of the Act's educational legislation. Although sections 7 and 8 were significant structural breakthroughs in 1944, their success, imagined by the Act's architects, was tied to changes being made in educational philosophy through the promotion of Christian-civic humanism. Although this philosophy was suggested in section 7's language, details for Christian-civic humanism in English education were spelled-out in sections 25-30, "Religious Education in County and Voluntary Schools; and sections 41-47, "Further Education." Sections 25-30 mandated Religious Education—a historic educational decree. More specifically, section 25 stated that every county and voluntary school would begin each day with "collective worship" and that each school would require "religious instruction" for its students (20-21). Sections 41-47 on further education, as well as sections 53 and 56 ("Supplementary Provisions") detailed landmark plans for widespread and diverse further education including youth services and educational training outside of formal school settings. The most important sections of the Act, then, included more than plans for re-structuring elementary and secondary education or "secondary education for all," but offered additional policy and philosophy for how national education should be provided for commonweal.

As part of that broader framework, Religious Education was clearly stated as a main tenet of the Act. Section 7, which defined the three stages of the system, not only stated that the "duty" of each LEA within those three stages was to contribute to "spiritual [and] moral" development but the Act's language gave these duties precedence over the duty for "mental" development (4).

The Act's key section on Religious Education, with several goals, stated,

> The school day in every [state] school and in every voluntary school shall begin with collective worship on the part of all pupils in attendance at the school, and the arrangements made therefore shall provide for a single act of worship attended by all pupils . . . [and] religious instruction shall be given in every [state] school and in every voluntary school (20-24).

The 1944 Act's Religious Education sections served ecumenical—and political—goals by bringing burgeoning English citizens together in an act of Christian communal worship. They also functioned as educational and financial compromises between church-run and state-run schools. At the same time, the mandate of Religious Education in the 1944 Act served a larger sacred socio-cultural purpose. Religious instruction and communal daily worship operated as spiritual and ideological buttresses against radical revolutionary trends that were perceived as threatening twentieth-century England. For Butler, Clarke, Mannheim and their colleagues, a daily reaffirmation of Christian ethics would reinforce what Butler had called the foundation stones of English culture in an era of "rapid and pervasive change" (1952).

The Religious Education mandate, then, was more than simply an effort to revive or maintain Christian church rolls in England. Christian values, particularly ideals of Christian brother- and sisterhood and community, served Butler's remarkable plans for using education in the reconstruction of society at large. The reformed educational system would help the English society remain steady in times of flux by keeping it rooted in solid English traditions and national character. It would also provide moral guidance for a progressive, yet diversified, economy. Christian fellowship would support progressive national economic growth by limiting the evils of "Economic Man"—alienation and exploitation—and help to transcend the cultural-vocational divide through a spirit of Christian community.

Theoretically, Christian mores applied to an industrial democracy could help to soften socio-economic divides by promoting ethics that served the common good. By promoting this cultural spirit, diverse education leading to a highly educated and trained workforce could enable England to act competitively and compassionately on the world stage. Professional and practical workers would be united by a Christian brother- and sister hood serving the English commonweal. So while the emerging superpowers, the United States and the Soviet Union, embraced and promoted secular systems of schooling as most productive for the twentieth century, under Butler's plans England would maintain its religious tradition as part of cultural education, and as a social support for its industrialized democracy. This was not an attempt to placate the masses with a cultural opiate, but a promise to preserve aspects of traditional English culture and morality which traditionalists and progressives believed could serve the community as a philosophical tether of justice, democracy, and Christian community.

Although the 1944 Act did not refer to religious instruction or Religious Education as Christian by name, Parliamentary debates, church declarations, educational reports, and the popular press had indicated and agreed that Christianity was the meaning behind the bill's legislation on Religious Education. In section 29 the Act stipulated that local educational authorities, teachers, and representatives from Anglican and Non-conformist churches, would draw up, or adopt from another LEA, a "non-denominational" "Agreed Syllabus" for Religious Education (24-25). English church, government and school officials had long defined and interpreted "denomination" as a recognized branch of English Christianity.

Conventional wisdom on English religious life in the 1940s suggested that an ecumenical, non-denominational, Christianity represented the nation's religious core. The 1940s emphasis on a specifically Christian Religious Education in England was based on a contemporary understanding of a traditional and solid foundation for English culture and mores. C. A. Alington, headmaster of Eton, for example, argued in his 1942 study, *Christianity in England: An Historical Sketch*, "The English character has been built up on that [Christian] foundation" (187). The piece was republished in 1943 and 1946 suggesting its continued relevance. E. O. James, a historian and philosopher of religion, affirmed the essential "social function of religion" in England in his 1940 *The Social Function of Religion*. Alington's and James' assessments of the national character and social purposes of religion closely paralleled the Christian-civic humanism of politicians like Butler and educationalists such as Clarke.

As a safeguard, the 1944 Act followed earlier precedents in religious instruction, including clauses stating that parents could request that their children be excused from religious worship at school, religious instruction at school, or both. A catch-22 to these clauses was section 25 of the 1944 Act, which stipulated that students who did not receive religious instruction during the school day were required to receive it elsewhere, putting a burden on parents and students to find a time and place for Religious Education outside school hours. Given the confusing and detailed requirements and the burdens opting-out of Religious Education put on parents, students, clergy, and schools, the London County Council records and Fabian Brigid Brophy (1967), for example, noted that many parents outside the Christian fold simply allowed their children to attend the school's Religious Education program.

The difficulties and stigmas of opting out benefitted the underlying goals of religious assembly. Educationalists interpreted the goals of religious assembly as two-fold. Although Religious Education obviously was meant to provide students with "grounding in the principles of the Christian faith as it ought to be practiced in this country," as noted in a 1954 "Report of an Inquiry made by the Research Committee of the Institute of Christian Education in the Working of the 1944 Education Act" entitled *Religious Education in Schools,* it was also meant to promote a corporate feeling in the schools between students and teachers (xi). Thus opting-out became even less attractive in an educational climate rooted in ideas of the school community. As the only time each school day that the entire school came together, missing the act of corporate worship was not merely missing Christian prayers, but meant, as scholar Gregory Dochuk has argued, alienation from the school community (2006), and was, thus, something to be avoided.

Indeed, social critics raised little commotion against the Religious Education edicts of the 1944 Act. On the subject of religious instruction, for example, in 1944-45, Lady Shena Simon, the prominent socialist educationalist, social reformer, Manchester "mayoress" and city council member wrote an analysis of the 1944 Act for the Fabian Society. Lady Simon's critical reading circled, but did not probe, the historic Religious Education mandate. She did argue, "If the new conditions of a compulsory act of worship and compulsory religious teaching, work to the detriment of complete freedom of conscience of teachers, there will be much more lost in the moral sphere than will have been gained" (15-16). Yet her commentary focused simply on administrative and legal issues. Simon's anxiety that the religious mandate might affect the hiring of a diverse teaching staff crucial to a [reformist] progressive educational system was a valid concern. Nevertheless, Simon's overall lack of attention to the deeper socio-cultural meanings behind Religious Education mandate suggests she did not question the meaning of [Christian] Religious Education for the nation's youth as a whole, so long as individual teachers' rights were not trampled upon. Simon was hardly alone in her glancing critique. In fact, outside of small and specifically anti-religious organizations such as the Rationalists, protest against the mandate of Religious Education was virtually non-existent. If protest against Religious Education was virtually mute, textbook authors gave ringing support to the Religious Education mandate and its Christian-civic humanism as embedded in the 1944 Act.

Religious textbooks published in the years surrounding the passage of the 1944 Religious Education mandate emphasized Christian-civic humanism with four major themes: England's history as a Christian nation; Christianity as the only just, honorable, and moral belief system; Christianity as the only modern and civilized belief system; and the necessity for English citizens to learn about Christianity. These arguments were made with zealous if not proselytizing messages of faith. More importantly, they also presented the trope of Christianity as a peculiar English characteristic and as a means of providing moral and social structures and philosophy akin to that envisioned by architects of the 1944 Act such as Butler and Clarke. James argued, for example, that, "Christianity can never fulfill its proper function till it becomes the integrative and directive force in human life shaping history in accordance with divine purpose" (302-303). His text, the 1940 and 1948 *The Social Function of Religion*, examined themes that fit closely with the messages of other Christian intellectuals encouraging formal Religious Education in schools.

James' textbook included discussions of "ethics and morality," "the Church and the community," "the nation and nationalism," as well as "religion and the modern world." He argued specifically for the need to return to and strengthen "foundations" in society such as religion while criticizing the methods of totalitarian leaders who followed quasi-religious models but provided false idols, dialectics, and "perverted standard[s] of values" (viii). Finally, James proposed that Christianity be integrated within the modern state to meet the challenges of the modern world. He argued that its "philosophical and theological presuppositions must be recognized," and that "[if] a religious system of values is to become the guiding principle of our civilization, religion like science must be regarded as an essential element in modern education and general culture" (299-306). This included recommendations for how to approach Religious Education in schools and universities.

Alington's "historical sketch," *Christianity in England,* (1942; 1943; 1946), echoed James' work arguing that the foundation of English character had been built upon English Christianity. He stated that the war had catalyzed a basic test of Christian versus un-Christian characters with England's "enemies" failing to uphold "freedom," "justice," and "truth and honor between nations" (187). The war revealed the "Christian influence" in the lives of many who did not call themselves Christian but had embraced Christian virtues and ethics during the war: Alington argued, "We are [all] fighting for great causes" (187). One of these causes, he explained, was the "freedom to think and worship," but his sketch suggested that for England this freedom was tied to "the belief in the Christian God which has fixed these ideas or ideals [justice, freedom, truth, and honor] in our hearts" (187). Alington feared that English history and tradition were threatened by the challenges of the war and enemies' "un-Christian character." Christians and those with Christian virtues, Alington contended, would ultimately succeed.

In relation to calls for invigorated Religious Education, A. C. Toyne, a "teacher of religion" at Hele's School in Exeter, wrote in 1944 what he called "a plea for a revision of the syllabus" in *Religious Teaching for Schools*. Toyne argued that Religious Education could better reflect "the Christian Way of Life," rather than the standard yet narrow curriculum focus on what he called "the literature, history and geography of the Bible" (4-5). Toyne believed that Religious Education must focus less on Scriptural interpretation and study, "a collection of vague ideals and a study of [a] literary problem" and more seriously on "the Universe as a Moral Order in which Man has a high eternal destiny" (25). The focus on religious philosophy rather than rote learning would benefit students, teachers, and "national character" (Chapter 1 and pages 25 and 72). Toyne suggested that religion be taught as a way of life, not as a narrow, textual, reading of the Bible. The former method, he argued, was based on educational principles, not structural or materialist elements that seemed to interfere with modern pedagogy: "If the remarks in these pages take the thoughts of educationalists for a moment away from finance, control, status, denominationalism, grading, bricks and mortar, etc. and turn them to Education itself, then many earnest and anxious assistant teachers, I know, will be grateful" (4-5). Toyne linked this to pedagogical guidance he referred to as "the ends," not the means, of education. Toyne's pleas paralleled the arguments of Butler and Clarke in pressing for education that would promote national character and a national educational philosophy in the form of a traditional English cultural medium: Christian religious spirit and values.

Despite these shared concerns for Christian cohesion at the national level, under English education law local education authorities could, and did, claim a large amount of control over their schools, their curriculum, and their students, based on local population and local concerns. Thus, in 1944, each LEA held some power to shape Religious Education within its own schools as stated by the 1944 Act's section 29.2. The London County Council (LCC), for example, used the 1944 Act's Religious Education mandate as an opportunity to revise and expand London's Religious

Education syllabus. The LCC and its Education Office redesigned Religious Education in its schools to meet the demands of the 1944 Act and its own educational community through its 1947 "The London Syllabus of Religious Education." The new London Syllabus was less pluralistic than its earlier iteration.

The London County Council had a reputation as a progressive education authority. As the heart of the British Empire, London comprised a diverse population and was compelled to engage in social experimentations that smaller or more insular populations across the nation escaped. London was also the urban and cultural center of England, attracting progressive groups such as the Fabians and the Bloomsbury Group which led to early blossoming of conditions favorable toward progressive forms of education. In addition, London had a distinct, if not ironic, advantage after the Second World War. The destruction of the city's schools during the Blitz allowed London officials to use the war as a catalyst to literally and figuratively rebuild the educational system from the ground up, as noted by London County Council officials.

The London County Council saw government calls for reform of Religious Education as an excellent opportunity to redraft their own agreed syllabus for religion, since the existing syllabus was a "brief" and "bare outline" of only three pages. The older syllabus was broad enough, however, to include an appendix of religious instruction approved for Jewish children. In September 1941, a report by the London Education Committee's chief inspector, J. Browne, suggested that although the London syllabus was still in use by over 50 percent of the Council's schools, more recent syllabi, such as those published in Cambridgeshire and Yorkshire, were "[more] comprehensive and detailed documents," and a new Council syllabus "would undoubtedly create fresh interest and impetus." The reputation of the LCC within England, and documents related to LCC revision of Religious Education during the war, suggested that London's new religious syllabus would contain progressive religious pedagogy, including moves toward multi-faith education to serve the city's religious diversity.

The new London Syllabus of Religious Education (LSRE), published in 1947 after two years of intensive research and discussion did not reflect this observation *in toto*. The syllabus incorporated progressive Christian thinking, but it did not embrace multi-faith, including secular faith, concerns. Indeed, having lost its appended Jewish lesson plans, the LSRE presented a progressive Religious Education, yet in a completely Christian framework. The final syllabus was in contrast to the London County Council's Education Officer's wartime caveats about blatant Christian-biased Religious Education in relation to the rights of teachers, children, and parents, particularly those of minority religious faiths. The new syllabus, however, was in line with the national trends embodied in contemporary legislation and pedagogy—including the 1944 Act.

The LSRE was initiated, at least in part, during the 1941 "Conference on Religious Education" which included representatives from Christian clergy—both the Church of England and the Free Churches—teachers' associations, and the London County Council. The introduction to the syllabus, written by The Right Rev. F. A. Cockin, D.D., The Lord Bishop of Bristol, a member of the conference, and a noted collaborator in the Christian Education Movement and the *Christian News-Letter*, reflects the deep thought and progressive, if Christian-based, trends that went into the development of the syllabus and the national mandate of Religious Education. Some of the issues and trends Cockin introduced included: Questions about what religious instruction *is*; the history and development of Biblical interpretation, from Allegorical to post-critical; and the intellectual and emotional sophistication necessary for teaching religion in the nation's schools. His introduction revealed a sophisticated discussion of Religious Education and its meaning for modern England. These questions and analysis confirmed that the LCC understood the trends that were shaping the 1944 Act: Progressive thought must be firmly rooted in Christianity, reflecting the construction of Religious Education for *Christian*-civic humanism rather than for multi-faith Religious Education.

The LSRE reflected the LCC's interest in the trends of progressive and civic-minded pedagogy. Religious Education plans were based on child-centered teaching, integrated curriculum, and attempts to bring curriculum content up-to-date with students' personal lives. This thinking permeated the syllabus, particularly within the sections geared toward secondary school students. The syllabus' suggestions for school assembly, for example, recommended that students be made to feel that they could make a personal contribution to assembly and worship. Curriculum guidelines for students in secondary schools included religious instruction integrated with critical thinking, historical and literary interpretation, current social trends, and preparation for "adult life" (67-70).

Yet if Religious Education for Jewish and other religious minority children was to be continued, as indicated by earlier war-era LCC discussions and documents, this content and curriculum was missing in the new syllabus. In fact, the only mention of other religions within the 1947 London syllabus were references to early Judaism in connection to early Christian history, and a short history section entitled, "Religions Contemporary With Christianity," which contained brief summaries of "early religions," Judaism and the "Mystery religions" of the Roman Empire, as well as "Eastern religions," including Hinduism, Buddhism, Islam, Confucianism, Taoism, and Shintoism (29). The syllabus contained no suggestions for alternative syllabi, worship, or Religious Education for children who were not Christian or not religious, nor for students whose parents requested that they be exempted from Religious Education as allowed in the 1944 Act. The emphasis was clearly on a Christian community with Christian ethics. The political and intellectual emphases on the need for a unified philosophy—Christian ethics—within the schools had permeated from the Board of Education, Parliament, and Christian leaders to reshape the Agreed Syllabus of the leading—and arguably most progressive—educational authority in the nation.

The LSRE is a symbol of the historic 1944 mandate for Religious Education as a moment of affirmation of Christian identity, not just an expedient compromise between sects. Politicians and educationalists meant Christian Religious Education to bolster the English against the moral and spiritual malaises caused by modern warfare. Daily collective worship would create a cohesive cultural community within schools and subsequently spread to a wider English Christian culture. Butler made clear that with educational reform he had meant to promote "the inheritance of [a non-debased] culture," clarified as, "enshrine[ing] for the future in English educational law the ancient and unalterable truth that the fear of the Lord is the beginning of knowledge" (1952, 43). Through Religious Education, Christian ethics were presented to youth as crucial to maintaining English national character in the postwar world.

The Religious Education mandate stipulated by the 1944 Act was maintained throughout the twentieth century yet its intellectualized Christian-civic meanings were subdued within a decade of the Act's passage. Although the London County Council and its Education Officer's department implemented the 1947 syllabus, by 1955, for example, minutes from a March 17 LCC Consultative Council on Educational Matters meeting included a suggestion that every secondary school child should be provided with a Bible "for his [*sic*] own use," and to keep after "he" left school. Members suggested that the Bible "not be regarded as just another text book," but gave no recommendations for how this was to be accomplished or what deeper meaning the Bible held. The Committee generally agreed that Bibles should be presented to each child upon leaving school. This LCC council saw the Christian Bible as a holy object to be "treasure[d]" by children in and out of school, but not, based on their conversations, as a pedagogical device to be used as part of a deeper exploration of Christian ethics. This kind of ritualized rather than spiritual

Religious Education was expressly the kind of uninspired Religious Education that educators like Toyne abhorred and had warned against. By calling the Bible a "prize" the LCC Council demoted the book to a symbol rather than a fundamental tool in earlier Religious Educationalists' goals to help students discover, as Toyne had suggested, the "moral order" of the "universe" in development of their "national character" (1944, 4-5). This episode was foreshadowing of postwar religious educationalists' missed opportunities to carry forward philosophical Christian-civic curriculum.

In 1962, for example, at the request of the Primary and Secondary Schools Sub-Committee, a survey of Religious Education in London schools was conducted by the Education Officer's department. The main concern of the survey was to determine if the "minimum requirements" of the Religious Education mandates of the 1944 Act were attended to in the London school system, including state and voluntary schools. Results of the survey revealed educationalists' foci on standards and curriculum rather than pedagogical assessment. The report found that most schools met for a daily act of worship; however, an average of only one hour per week was allocated to religious instruction, not including classes devoted to studying for the General Certificate of Education exam in religion, in which cases Religious Education classes could include up to six periods per week. The report suggested, as well, that while Religious Education maintained a Protestant-Christian bias, Christian-based Religious Education and communal forms of worship were failing to create a national spirit.

A March 7, 1962 article in the *Daily Telegraph and Morning Post*, "Restoring Morals to the Curriculum," made even clearer that philosophical goals of Religious Education as imagined by the 1944 Act were failing. Despite the increased presence of Religious Education in schools since the 1944 Act, the article's author F. H. Hilliard argued, "school-leavers often make it abundantly plain that they do not see much connection between religion and life." Religious Education had largely manifested itself in rote learning, rather than as a philosophical examination meant to help promote national unity. As such, it seemed that Religious Education had missed its opportunity to provide a basis for an educational philosophy suggested by architects of the 1944 Act. These perceived failures opened Religious Education to increasingly critical and dismissive arguments in the decades to come. Postsecular scholars have begun to reexamine Religious Education's effect on postwar England. Special attention should be paid to the fact that the mandate of Religious Education, with a Christian bias, remained a legislative requirement in English schools and was reaffirmed, with explicit references to its

Christian character, in the 1988 Education Act. Interest in Religious Education as a means of social cohesion also saw a resurgence after 9/11.

Until 9/11 relatively few studies examined the larger historical and cultural meanings of the Act's religious provisions which mandated the "spiritual [and] moral . . . development of the community," beyond some basic analyses of the relationships between the churches and the state. This silence extended to scholarly analysis and criticism of Religious Education in schools. At least one such analysis argued that English Religious Education became a moot point by the 1960s, a theory now under reconsideration. In *Religion and Society in Twentieth-Century Britain* (2006) historian Callum Brown suggests, despite his assertion that "religion is back on the agenda," that Religious Education was insignificant because youth were no longer interested in the Christian faith and its continued place in mandated education was an anomaly (xv). The periodization of what Brown called "discursive Christianity"—marked by a precipitous drop-off in the 1960s—now seems too narrow with the benefits of twenty-first century hindsight. This now challenged historical periodization, as well as the consideration that post-1944 the Ministry of Education shifted from Conservative-led coalition government state welfare to Labour-led Welfare State policies, suggests reasons why the 1944 Religious Education mandate was regarded as insignificant in the mid- to late-twentieth century. Postsecular interpretation allows historians to reexamine why Religious Education and collective worship in schools became and remains a mandated core subject in the national curriculum. As the Office for Standards in Education, UK, (Ofsted) noted in "Making Sense of Religion," (2007) it was now time to ask how Religious Education had influenced students and culture after the 1944 mandate—and after 9/11.

In their extremely concise yet powerful analysis of the 1988 Educational Reform Act, with its necessary references to the legislation of the 1944 Act, Edwin Cox and Josephine M. Cairns provided early insight for the "opportunit[ies] missed" following the legislation of the 1944 Act and opportunities missed in evaluating its historical significance (1989). Cairns argues that post-1944 the Act's educational proposals were "narrowly conceived," "a mismatch with the reality of the classroom and the intentions of the legislators" (10-11). Postsecular thought reveals that interpretations of the 1944 Act which glossed over its promotion of Christian ethics were also narrowly conceived and thus reexamining the Act through a lens of its traditional social welfare—civic—interpretations *and* its Christian tenets provide compelling interpretations.

CHAPTER SEVEN

FURTHER EDUCATION FOR ALL?

> The statutory system of public education shall be organised in three progressive stages to be known as primary education, secondary education, and further education . . .
> —*Education Act 1944*, c. 31, Part II, Section 7

Civic-mindedness, including the understanding of the duties and rights of officials and acknowledgement of the duties and rights of citizens within Education complemented the spiritual philosophies of the 1944 Education Act with respect for the material interests of the nation. The relationship between Religious Education and this civic education was envisioned as symbiotic. "Further Education," a key but often marginalized section of the 1944 Act, supplemented and echoed the historic statements for secondary education for all. In sub-sections 41-47, "Further Education" outlined the responsibilities of local educational authorities (LEAs), schemes of further education, as well as other administrative and interim provisions to continue the development of proactive, engaged citizens *after* students' secondary education had ended.

A number of sections of the 1944 Act spelled out duties and rights in secondary and further education, youth services, and youth employment. These sections and clauses pertained to the mandate of section 7 of the 1944 Act, which instructed LEAs to provide not just secondary, but also further, education according to the "needs of the population of their area." Within these edicts were the stated and implicit duties and rights of youth to avail themselves of secondary and further education opportunities that would allow them to best serve their own goals as well as the interests of their local and national communities.

In regard to section 7 of the 1944 Act—although egalitarian, comprehensive-style secondary education was an option, interwar educational thinking and advice indicated that secondary schooling was most effective for students and the nation when divided up into three types: grammar, technical, and modern schools. Politicians urged educationalists to base these separate schemes on logical divisions of resources according to students' aptitudes, abilities, and interests as the 1938 Spens and 1941 Norwood reports had recommended. The 1944 Act required each local educational authority to propose school systems based on local concerns and interests for Board of Education approval. Educational legislation allowed proposals with a variety of secondary school schemes: tripartite, multilateral, or comprehensive school structures. Comprehensives, however, were still considered experimental systems and would thus be practiced only under certain local conditions where the student body and local authority could best benefit from a comprehensive system. The Ministry of Education clarified this viewpoint in a 1945 report, "The Nation's Schools: Their Plan and Purpose." The London County Council (LCC), for instance, proposed a "London School Plan" comprehensive-style system in 1947 which they were allowed to develop.

Problems arose, however, in misunderstandings or disagreements between local and national visions of how secondary education for all should be administered. Some believed that a strict definition of comprehensive schooling meant that the nation as a whole must reject selection, tracking, or separation of students for any reason—thus limiting any bipartite or tripartite planning. Others argued that diversity was vital to serving the interests of local communities and resources. At the time, the importance of maintaining and developing local educational opportunities meshed with fears that overly-centralized state control could lead to tyranny. A *nationalized* comprehensive system was thus shied away from, yet secondary and further education for all was encouraged. Joan Thompson, an educationalist and member of the LCC, reported on LEA development plans stemming from the 1944 Act in her 1947 survey, "Secondary Education for All." She argued, "It must be remembered that LEAs vary very widely in the size, character, and resources of the areas under their control [and] many of the differences in the Development Plans are therefore the result of the different problems LEAs have to deal with" (5). These differences harkened back to a fundamental tenet of English culture and educational philosophy: individuality and autonomy. Nevertheless, they also involved more practical demographic and geographical concerns as well. Local areas, local populations, and local industries varied and thus so did their educational structures, aims, and opportunities.

While much national attention was focused on secondary education, the 1944 Act's sections 41-43 spelled out LEAs' duties to provide "full-time and part-time education for persons over compulsory school age [fifteen]," as well as "leisure-time occupation, in such organized cultural training and recreative activities as are suited to their requirements." These "schemes of further education" were supplementary to additional plans to create "county colleges" within each local administrative area to provide further education for "young persons who are not in full-time attendance at any school or other educational institution." County college instruction would encompass "practical physical and vocational training, as will enable [young people] to develop their various aptitudes and capacities and will prepare them for the responsibilities of citizenship." These sections laid out explicit assertions to officials and students that education and training was a civic duty to prepare students for their adult roles as citizens.

The 1944 Act envisioned attendance in county colleges or within another scheme of further education as mandatory for all students. Terms of attendance could vary, however, according to each individual student's needs, position, and schedule. Students past the compulsory school age—the 1944 Act recommended age 15—who had gained employment, for example, could effectively count college attendance hours within their "computation of working hours" stated the 1944 Act's section 60, so as to limit their hours of work and study to prevent overburdening daily life. Section 44 noted that young people attending other educational institutions, including universities, as well as those who trained in the merchant marines or sea fishing industry, were exempt from county college attendance. In addition, students could gain exemption from attending on days of religious observances and holidays (section 44).

In principle, however, attendance in some form of further education in county colleges was expected for all young persons between the ages of fifteen and eighteen to serve their educational and cultural needs in becoming well-rounded adult citizens. Attendance in other voluntary continuation education programs was permissible if an LEA agreed the education was "suitable and efficient" (sections 42, 44, and 81.) In addition to the sections specifically outlining compulsory plans for further education, youth services, and county colleges, each LEA was directed to provide "facilities for recreation and social and physical training," either within "community centres" or by use of existing facilities in coordination with voluntary bodies (section 53). County colleges, as well, would become part of the local educational community serving the needs of the local population.

Each local plan would, however, be subject to review and approval by national authorities (sections 8-13, 23, and 24). The language and details of further education and youth services related to employment and leisure within the 1944 Act were limited to some degree by the legislative jargon and legal rhetoric inherent to such a document. Nonetheless, as was the case with the 1944 Act's statements on Religious Education, a variety of supplementary information and guidance was published on infrastructure, organization, and philosophy for secondary and further education. These documents related specifically to aspects of further education, the youth services, and non-formal or non-traditional educational opportunities. These included official and private publications such as *The Nation's Schools: Their Plan and Purpose* (1945), "Report of the Committee on the Juvenile Employment Service," (1945); *The Education Act: A Parents' Guide*, (1946); and the book, *For Youth Only*, released in 1949.

This literature provided guidelines for secondary and further education. Again, the impetus remained with LEAs to make local decisions on organization, curriculum, and allocation of students. Because the national government respected individual liberty and local autonomy, they attempted to consolidate and reform secondary and further education without nationalizing its content and authority. Thus, when the Workers' Education Association criticized the 1944 Act in their 1947 "Secondary Education for All: Some Problems Discussed," arguing, "Nowhere in the Act is there any indication as to how the provision of secondary education according to these principles [full time education suitable to the requirements of senior pupils . . . [ages] 12-19] is to be organised," its members were missing the point (3). The scope of supplementary works was impressive and was meant to guide educationalists and the general public as to the 1944 Act's possibilities in local arenas for secondary and further education, rather than stipulate nationalized requirements.

The 1945 Ministry of Education's *The Nation's Schools: Their Plan and Purpose* discussed both the relative merits and disadvantages of various types of schools and organizational plans, while urging a variety of schemes. In *The Nation's Schools* the Ministry argued: "Tradition [is] to keep our schools more intimate communities (x)." The Ministry's statement allowed that, "in sparsely populated districts it may well be essential to bring together a variety of types of secondary course in one school unit so as to secure the numbers necessary for a proper school life" but they also agreed, "there is room for judicious experiment elsewhere before we can feel any confidence that we know what is best for the children (22-23)." This caution for comprehensive re-organization on a national level had educational and pedagogic claims, given that at the time comprehensive schooling was, for England, radical, foreign, and experimental. Yet progressive school organizations, such as comprehensives, were not beyond the pale. Official caution in reforming educational systems nation-wide did not, for example, prevent the London County Council's comprehensive proposal or proposals for ten multilateral schemes in their 1947 "London School Plan."

Political and educational rhetoric guided reform of school structures and educational policies. The size of secondary schools and classroom populations, for example, remained a crucial educational and pedagogic concern for educationalists. The issue also carried cultural undertones in terms of educationalists' plans to create or maintain a sense of community within the schools. Politicians and parents had already expressed concern about class size in relation to the value of received education. Professional wisdom at the time—including the Spens Report and the Ministry's *The Nation's Schools*—argued that smaller classes were better for students and better served the school community as a whole. As the Spens Report noted, students learned to know one another, their teachers, and their head better in smaller school population environments. Thus, educational research on school populations, as well as conventional wisdom, guided decision-making about educational reconstruction and reform.

In relation to educational research, continuing fears and anxiety that nationalization would result in regimented and over-populated schools working as educational mills ensured that larger schools, particularly comprehensives, remained limited and experimental. Surveys and analysis of comprehensive systems in the United States, the Soviet Union, and Sweden did little to calm anxieties because education was regarded as a socio-cultural activity unique to each nation, if not each locality. The Council for Curriculum Reform, an independent association of educationalists, argued that information regarding experimentation in education was badly needed in the English sphere. The group agreed in the 1945 "The Contents of Education" that in the English sphere this information was "exiguous," forcing researchers to turn to American sources. Nonetheless, the Council argued, "It is not always possible to apply to one social scene the results obtained in another" (10). Thus, English educationalists believed they must find their own path for school structures and systems. This would take time.

In the decades following the 1944 Act, Ministry of Education official correspondence and reports urged careful deliberation and further investigation, research, and limited local experimentation with comprehensive systems before developing them as a national system. These documents, most now housed in the National Archives, include a plethora of interesting commentary on a myriad of issues related to education and society in general including: public and parental biases toward forms of secondary schools; educationalist, teacher, and head attitudes toward comprehensive, grammar, and technical schools; local variations in populations and employment opportunities; concerns about the size of individual school populations and the educational effects therein; and debates over "selection" methods and transfers of students between various secondary schools. The bottom line for the government was that local educational systems serve the needs of local populations and local youth, rather than international educational or psychological trends.

Testing and examinations used to gauge student aptitude had gained legitimacy during the interwar era based on the growing professional field of educational psychology and perceived efficiency of such measurements. Yet educationalists, psychologists, and politicians associated with the making of the 1944 Act were keenly aware that educational and vocational psychology could serve only as tools and guidelines, not decisive methods of selection and allocation for students. As tools, they were meant to help guide teachers, parents, and children in making careful decisions for school-choice, rather than dividing children by abstract ideas about intelligence. It should be noted that the popularity and professional use of these types of intelligence and vocational testing continued in the postwar era.

Thus, proposals surrounding the 1944 Act for school diversity and the separation of children to attend varied grammar, technical, or modern schools were not meant to be based on separation of students by their abstract intelligences. Critics suggested that intelligence tests were designed to decide which students were academically versus practically minded. This, however, was not meant as a judgment call that elevated the social relevance of academic work over practical work. Butler had argued, for example, in his 1942 speech to the NUT, that school allocation should be based on a myriad of educational evaluations, as well as parental wishes, and the aptitudes, abilities, and interests of the child. The national government was encouraging LEAs to look for children whose practical-minded characteristics made them likely, willing, and motivated candidates for technical and modern educational tracks. This was not a plan for demoting or degrading students—in the language of educationalists—whose abilities, interests, and aptitudes suggested their strengths lay in practical skills and industrial, domestic, or technical vocations. Rather, politicians and educationalists sought out students who had aptitudes and interests geared toward doing essential agricultural, industrial, and technical work that would best benefit the students' interests and the nation's productivity. It is worth repeating the sentiment expressed in the Commons on February 9, 1944: "We have to raise the status of the fellow who works in overalls higher than that of the man who wears a black coat and a white collar and sits in an office." A viable commonwealth required a variety of trained and educated professionals and workers. In addition, the educational system could not assume that all students desired the same type of education. The 1945 pamphlet, *The Nation's Schools: Their Plan and Purpose*, argued many of these points succinctly,

> It has been suggested that [provision for 'three broad types' of student] can be determined by a percentage formula based on normal distribution of different kinds of ability. Such a formula may be a useful general check or guide, but can hardly be of universal application. The conditions and requirements of different areas will vary . . . Secondary education in an area should be envisaged as a whole consisting of different types, the balance between which may be altered as the needs of pupils, the wishes of parents and local requirements become clearer in course of time. Fundamentally we have to select schools for children not children for schools (13).

If the first step was selecting schools for children, a second was helping students find appropriate and meaningful work in their post-secondary and adult lives.

In this regard, the Ministry worked to align youth education with employment opportunities. Two earlier reports, "Youth Service After the War," and "Teachers and Youth Leaders," published in formal association with the Board of Education, had highlighted the socio-cultural provisions of a planned youth service. Government officials had also initiated plans to bring education closer to the world of juvenile employment. The "Report of the Committee on the Juvenile Employment Service," published by the Ministry of Labour and National Service in 1945, symbolized the creation and joint administration of a Juvenile Employment Service, although ministerial responsibility remained within the Ministry of Labour. The key functional and philosophical guideline of this service was to "play its part in helping the boy and girl in their passage from school to the world of adult independence" (12). Although the report noted the importance of both education and recreation in the lives of young people, it also stated clearly, "the pivot of the life of almost every boy and girl who has left school is the job" (12). Hence, the service would provide vocational guidance for all school-leavers up to age 17, including those from private schools. The goal, again, was to help youth find employment suited to their interests and abilities, taking into consideration their school records, parents' wishes, and the needs of local and national employment trends.

The service was not put in place as a means of control over work or industry. Many of its functions were imagined as informational and as guidance to ease young people into the world of work, adulthood, and citizenship. For example, the Committee's report recommended juvenile service officers follow juveniles' progress after they had taken a job and the report suggested the practice of an "open evening," at local Juvenile Employment offices so young workers could seek further help or guidance as necessary (24-25). In addition, the Juvenile Employment Committee recommended further training schemes through scholarships for further training or "apprenticeships" (28). A system for "re-placing in employment," was also considered for young workers who were unhappy in their work or who were ready to move to "more suitable employment" (24). In addition, the committee suggested that juvenile employment services and officers create close connections with schools to provide students with information about choosing a career and to give them hands-on opportunities to explore the world of work and various occupations.

The Committee viewed these services as connections between formal secondary and further education and the world of work and schemes that would become "[a] normal teaching [function] of a school" (1). Schools would provide opportunities to students and school-leavers to "see industrial plants, firms, exhibitions" films, and "school talks," as aids toward eventual choices for careers (17). The report made a pointed argument, however, that "care [be] taken at this stage to keep the child's mind open" to a variety of careers (17). As well, despite the report's clear indications of an assumed population decline, especially of juvenile workers, the Committee strongly recommended, "that it is not desirable to institute any system of compulsory control of engagements for juveniles . . . this would be wrong and wholly unacceptable to public opinion" (22). The key, rather, was to provide education, guidance, and support for young people. Thus, the civic goals of bridging the cultural-vocational divide were made apparent in community-based efforts to provide further education and youth services for individual cultural and vocational development for commonweal.

The reports discussed above were written by and largely meant for an audience of government officials and educationalists and may have been beyond the scope of some parents and members of the general public. More accessible publications, however, also discussed in detail the plans and proposals for further education. One such publication, the 1946 *The Education Act: A Parents' Guide*, written by W. P. Alexander, with a foreword by R. A. Butler, was, obviously, directed at parents and a general public. In addition, Geoffrey Faber's publishing house released in 1949 *For Youth Only*. The book, written by Gordon Ette, a Youth Officer and official within the National Conference of Youth Service Officers of

England and Wales, served as an inspirational guide for potential youth leaders imagined to come from a variety of backgrounds and vocations. These publications not only made government plans and proposals more accessible to the general public, but reveal how these plans maintained official and public interest in the potential of the 1944 Act after its passage.

Butler's foreword and Alexander's introduction to *A Parents' Guide*, for example, stated their purpose as "open[ing] a new chapter in the history of education" in England by including parents and students in a discussion about the new educational policies and philosophies (3). Using, "more direct language" than the education legislation, W. P. Alexander set forth "the major provisions of the 1944 Act with special emphasis on those parts important to parents" (iv). He wrote concise and well-organized sections so that the entire pamphlet ran to only thirty-nine pages. In addition, the pamphlet excluded confusing and convoluted legislative jargon as well as sections that clearly pertained to administrative bureaucracy rather than parents of students. Butler's foreword to the guide gave legitimacy to the parents' pamphlet tied to his role as former Minister of Education. Butler indicated his clear approval of the pamphlet, and reiterated for anxious parents the rationale behind the slow time-frame expected for the 1944 Act's implementation. Butler reminded parents that, "in the words of the present Minister of Education, [the 1944 Education Act will] 'take a whole generation to bring into force.'" (v). This statement emphasized the evolutionary, rather than revolutionary, essence of the 1944 Act.

Butler's foreword to *A Parents' Guide* also contained a key statement indicating the overall progressive spirit of the publication and the legislation it described: "The intention of the Act was to give to skill in hand and eye the same opportunity and the same status as is at present afforded to excellence in the sphere of academic studies" (v). Alexander followed the spirit of this introduction in his detailed explanation of the 1944 Act. Alexander also promoted another key theme: "parental choice" as a right and a responsibility. He made special note of the 1944 Act's directive to parents to procure for their children "efficient full-time education suitable to [your child's] age, ability and aptitude" (2). In terms of rights, the key section of *A Parent's Guide* devoted to "further education" was subtitled "a plan for everybody" echoing the ideals of secondary education for all (14).

The guide's advice to parents included careful consideration of the various kinds of further education available. This section was significant, as it suggested how rights and responsibilities in education intertwined.

Alexander argued that university or other formal higher education was only one path for students. The university track, despite its social prestige, benefitted some but not all young people's interests and abilities (14-15). Alexander described further educational paths that paralleled the university in guiding students to further education and potential careers but did not require full-time dedication to academics. In this vein, the guide provided information on facilities for "voluntary higher education" as well as compulsory further education. Alexander reminded parents that under the 1944 Act, LEAs had a responsibility to provide a variety of further education schemes for young people including technical, commercial, artistic, vocational, and academic training.

As a practical service to parents, the guide discussed the costs of these various forms of further and higher education. Although compulsory county colleges would be free, universities and other forms of voluntary higher education could charge fees. A system of scholarships and financial assistance, however, was to be put in place so that "any child who has sufficient ability to take advantage of higher education in any form shall not be prevented from doing so by lack of means" (31). Thus, a system was envisioned in which all students had access, regardless of income, to full-time post-secondary education in addition to the part-time further education provided by county colleges and other youth services. The 1944 Act, then, actually went beyond secondary education for all—it stipulated further education for all.

Further education in the free county colleges, as mentioned above, *was* compulsory on a part-time basis for the juvenile school-leaver, and financial assistance could be provided by LEAs for students wishing to attend other forms of further education that required tuition fees. Alexander argued, "This provision of [compulsory, part-time, day attendance] at county colleges is not to be regarded as the forcing of the child back to school," an indication, in this guide for parents, that this right might be seen as a burdensome responsibility by parents eager to see their children entering paid employment (14). Rather, Alexander argued, the impetus of the county colleges was, "an endeavor to provide education up to eighteen for everybody, [and] recognition that . . . [for] many youngsters . . . [further] education . . . is best . . . a combination of . . . college and . . . work" (14-15). Thus, county colleges opened up alternatives for students who saw their future outlined outside full-time university higher education. The county colleges would provide a variety of courses geared toward "special technical training," as well as courses and activities meant to improve intellectual, practical, and leisure-time pursuits for life-long learning.

In a time when demographic decline appeared to be a stark reality, young people past the age of compulsory education served as a crucial part of the economic sector of society, both within industry, and within their own family units. Politicians, educationalists, and employers, however, recognized that training youth to serve local and national economies was only one part of their education as future citizens. Thus, Alexander explained to parents how part-time continuation education would cultivate young people's growth toward full adulthood. Part-time continuation education benefitted employers, parents, and educationalists by providing young people with some discipline in addition to further education: "An [educational] combination of theory and practice . . . and . . . the need to keep these young people under supervision and guidance in the early stages of their careers" (14-15). Young people would benefit as well by engaging in programs meant to expand their personal education and training, allowing them to begin to explore adult culture and society guided by trained and experienced youth officers and educators. At the same time, a connection between education and employment services would help guide young people into the world of work and prevent the exploitation of inexperienced workers by unscrupulous employers. An emphasis on culture and recreation within further education aimed to prevent young workers from becoming disenchanted in the world of work.

In this vein, the government expected to hire youth leaders to help develop cultural and vocational schemes in further education. A 1944 report by the Consultative Committee, which included Fred Clarke, "Teachers and Youth Leaders, (McNair)," had addressed "The Service of Youth" as well as a section on "Young People's Colleges," or county colleges. While acknowledging the anxieties of a "standardized" youth service, the report had firmly argued that, "when it is shown that voluntary effort cannot by itself cover the field and that therefore the service must be broader based and become a public responsibility, there is no escaping the fact that suitable persons must be encouraged to undertake the [youth] service as a profession" (94). The report had also stressed the need for the youth service to be "an integral part of the public service of education" on local and national levels. Within this framework, the committee recommended hiring between 5,000 and 6,000 youth leaders "from all walks of life" and making their salaries and pensions comparable with those of teachers (93-106).

The committee had made an assertive statement about the social and educative importance of the youth leaders: "those who by companionship and leadership aim at helping to meet the recreative, cultural, and spiritual needs of young people who are no longer in full-time attendance at school" (7). Following up on this report, the experienced youth leader, Gordon Ette, published *For Youth Only* with Faber & Faber, a study of the youth service dedicated to "[prospective] youth leaders and all concerned." In the spirit of the times, Ette emphasized youth service was tied to the characteristics of Christian values and citizenship, in opposition to the "subtle obstacle[s] of increasing comfort," and called for action through "a revitalized educational system, inspired and directed . . . [by] the Christian religion" (12). This call for action, Ette noted, remained rooted in a sense of liberty and individuality as well as a clear sense of the challenges, experiments, and spiritual fulfillment a future youth leader could expect in helping to shape the future of the nation through education and service to youth (Introduction and 13). These points conveniently echoed the underlying themes of Christian-civic humanism in education.

Written in part for the youth leader "still passing through the youth organizations of our country," Ette's guide was meant as inspiration not just to youth leaders, but to youth themselves, and the communities in which they lived, worked, and played (13). Thus, Ette also invoked the responsibilities of local communities, from home to school, from club to work, and of each individual, to create educated and socialized adults who would be able to practice autodidactism after formal guidance ended, thereby using critical analysis to navigate "a world of conflicting values" (Preface and 11). The crux of these educational guides extended the future of education beyond a simple restructuring of primary and secondary education suggested by narrower readings of sections 7 and 8 of the 1944 Act. Butler's 1944 Act's symbiotic system planned for and encouraged life-long learning schemes that bridged the gaps between academic and vocational and cultural and practical forms of education and training.

Regardless of the evidence for careful and thoughtful planning for youth services and further education as a means to better educate the nation, the historical record reveals that these plans for county colleges, youth services, and the effective administration and guidance of young workers, through programs like the Juvenile Employment Office, ultimately failed in the postwar era. The blame for these failures, however, is difficult to pin on the 1944 Act or its architects. Butler's influence at the Board of Education and in educational politics in general disappeared following the 1945 defeat of the coalition government to Labour. The postwar Labour government, meanwhile, faced a heavy economic burden in the aftermath of the war resulting in at least a decade of austerity and educational stagnation. Despite the shift to Labour leadership and their bold plans for a Welfare State, postwar politics and society moved cautiously as postwar malaise and Cold War rhetoric pointed English government officials toward cautious rather than radical reform. Specifically related to Butler-era education and youth service plans, however, Labour enacted changes in the Juvenile Employment Service which had a chilling effect on the development of youth services and further education.

A study conducted between 1958 and 1960 on the state of the youth service reported in "The Youth Service in England and Wales" (1960) that the 1945 (Labour) Ministry of Education put the McNair Committee recommendations for youth leaders on hold. Although discussions on providing youth services continued, "The Youth Service" report argued, "with one economic crisis after another the Ministry could do no more than indicate that the Youth Service and other forms of further education must be held back to allow" for more pressing educational concerns (5). This left the report's authors, including illustrious educational philosophers such as Richard Hoggart, to argue, "The Youth Service is at present in a state of acute depression" (1). Without attempting to shift blame on Labour's record from 1945 to 1951, or the Conservative record from 1951 to 1964, the report's authors suggested several reasons for these grim circumstances, including social, cultural, and demographic issues, as well as geographical inequalities (1). The Committee suggested that following the 1944 Act youth services had been neglected "both in educational circles and by public opinion generally" (1). Cultural and social trends continued to develop away from projects for youth services and vocational training so that by 1973, under Employment and Training Acts, registration for the Youth Employment Service was no longer compulsory. With this transition, youth employment services had been, at least symbolically, given the axe.

Formal further education in county colleges and other venues also failed. These failures were complex and also rooted in demographic, economic, and cultural issues. As early as 1947, Christopher Marsden had reported in *The Journal of Higher Education* that the Minister of Education had requested the LEAs to begin development plans for further education (365). Although Marsden attested his personal support for this system, he asked pointedly if such an "enormous project" was feasible at the time (365-6 and 392). His concerns centered on the ability of LEAs to handle this additional burden, given that school rolls had already increased as the school-leaving age now extended to fifteen, and that a lack of buildings and materials continued to plague the nation. These problems were exacerbated by continued shortages in England in the postwar years.

Analysis of the problems facing the creation of county colleges in the mid-1950s, such as Griffith William's 1955 "The First Ten Years of the

Ministry of Education," again cited continuing problems of lack of resources, finances, and the increase in school rolls from the extension of compulsory schooling and the postwar baby boom (103 and 109). He noted as well that increased burdens on educational administration in light of the 1944 Act, not to mention a general lack of "urgency" following the war, indicated a "decline in enthusiasm," for these further education projects (103 and 109). Williams also reported that although a policy thaw had begun after a "freeze-up" in the late 1940s, "there is still much confusion of thought on the question of principle whether adult education and the youth service are frills or necessities in the social community as it exists today" (108-9). Although proposals for part-time continuation colleges remained on the statute books until 1988, their lack of real development and overall failure was rooted in what scholar Penny Tinkler argued was "lack of consensus about [their] inherent value," compared to other reforms, and concerns over administration of the colleges" (2001, 94). Thus, social reconstruction through secondary and further education for all as envisioned by the architects of the 1944 Act failed. Plans for what Toyne termed an ethically-based Religious Education—"the Universe as a Moral Order in which Man has a high eternal destiny"—rather than one narrowly focused on "the literature, history and geography of the Bible" had also failed (1944, 4-5). J. M. Cairns and E. Cox argue succinctly,

> [T]he education system [following 1944] failed the newly emerging culture by not allowing its values to become conscious and to be expressed and celebrated. Had those opportunities been taken there might have arisen an educated post- [institutionalized] Christian democracy, conscious of its values, instead of one which gr[ew] confused, turbulent, and increasingly aggressive. A foundation might then have been laid for a reasoned and purposeful pluralism to take shape in the rapidly changing postwar community (1989, 12).

In the post-World War II-era these missteps interpreting and implementing Religious Education and further education, as well as the years of austerity, submerged educational philosophies as identified by Butler, Clarke, and Mannheim beneath secular working and middle-class concerns. By the time educational reform was put back on the front burner in the 1960s, educational politics and priorities had shifted from state welfare concerns to Labour-driven concerns for Welfare State policies in education. Stopgaps and shifting priorities in the aftermath of the 1944 Act thus resulted in decades of educational stagnation. Educationalists focused on bitter debates over whether or not nationalized, egalitarian, and comprehensive systems of education best served youth and the nation. In the wake of postwar austerity and class-driven debates over secondary education, Butler's 1944 Education Act's plan for variegated further education for burgeoning citizens married to the cohesive role of Religious Education—Christian-civic humanism as educational philosophy for England—was submerged and drowned.

GLOSSARY

People

Adams, William George Stewart.
In 1941 Adams formed the All Souls Group which served as an important and influential discussion group for leaders of education and others with comparable positions of authority. Members included: Fred Clarke; H. C. Dent, editor of the *Times Educational Supplement*; John Newsom; and guest R. A. Butler, President of the Board of Education.

Butler, Richard Austen.
As President of the Board of Education Butler organized and passed the 1944 Education Act in collaboration with the Board of Education, Parliament, the Anglican and Non-conformist churches, and a variety of educationalists, intellectuals, and Christian public servants including members of the Moot, the *Christian News-Letter* and the All Souls Group. Butler left public office at the age of 62 with one of the longest records of ministerial experience amongst contemporary politicians.

Clarke, Fred.
Clarke is credited as the principal founding father of the National Foundation for Educational Research, as well as having introduced a sociological lens into his own work and into English educational philosophy and research. This approach led to his influence on and consultation with intellectuals and educationalists in the Moot and the *Christian News-Letter*, and as correspondent/ consultant with the Conservative Sub-committees on Postwar Problems with special reference to the Sub-committee on Education and President of the Board of Education, R. A. Butler. Clarke's key publications include: *Essays in the Politics of Education* (1923) and *Education and Social Change, an English Interpretation*, (1940).

Eliot, Thomas Stearns (T. S.)
Eliot settled in England where he worked as a schoolmaster and a bank clerk, and eventually literary editor for the publishing house Faber & Faber. He later became a director at Faber & Faber and the founder and editor of *Criterion* (1922-1939). In 1927, Eliot became a British citizen and became a member of the Anglican Church. He served on President of the Board of Education, R. A. Butler's Conservative Committee on Postwar Problems with special reference to the Sub-committee on Education (1941); as a member of the Moot; and as a collaborator on the *Christian News-Letter*.

Faber, Geoffrey.
Faber served as chair of R. A. Butler's Conservative Sub-committee on Education (1941) and as a collaborator on the *Christian News-Letter*. Faber published a number of books on education and political education.

Mairet, Philip.
Mairet, a Swiss-born British journalist joined the Church of England and the Moot during World War II and also served as a collaborator on the *Christian News-Letter*.

Mannheim, Karl.
Born in Budapest, Mannheim held a position in the Hungarian Soviet in 1919 at the offer of his friend and teacher Georg Lukács. After the collapse of the government later that year, Mannheim moved to Germany and held academic posts at Heidelberg and Frankfurt until the first National Socialist enactments in 1933 suspended him from his posts. Mannheim came to England in 1933 as an exile from Germany. He was invited to take a position at the London School of Economics and quickly found a place within English academia and intelligentsia. By 1939, he had been invited to join the Moot, where he met Fred Clarke. Mannheim also served as a collaborator on the *Christian News-Letter* and served as an advisor to R. A. Butler's Conservative Committees on Postwar Problems with special reference to the Sub-committee on Education. In 1946 Fred Clarke asked Mannheim to serve as the first Chair of Sociology and Education at the Institute of Education, where Mannheim was a popular and influential teacher, a congenial and helpful colleague, and one who made significant contributions to the Institute and the study of education.

Moberly, Sir Walter H.
Moberly was a founder and core member of the Christian Frontier Council and the Moot; and a collaborator on the *Christian News-Letter*. Moberly wrote *The Crisis in the University* (1949), a well-received critical analysis of the universities.

Newsom, John.
Newson served as chair of the Central Advisory Council for Education, 1961, which produced the "Newsom Report" or "Half Our Future: Education of Pupils Aged 13-16 of Average or Less of Average Intelligence," which recommended raising the school leaving age to 16. He also served as chair of the Public Schools Commission, "Newsom Report on Public Schools" (1968) which explored ways public schools could be integrated with comprehensives. Newsom was a member of the All Souls Group and wrote *The Education of Girls*, 1948 with R. A. Butler contributing the preface and Faber & Faber as publisher.

Oakeshott, Walter F.
Oakeshott was a member of Butler's Conservative Sub-committee on Postwar Problems and collaborator on the *Christian News-Letter*.

Oldham, Joseph H.
A missionary and Christian educationalist, Oldham served as chair of the research committee for the Universal Christian Council for Life and Work (1934); organizer of the Oxford Conference (1937); and founded and edited the *Christian News-Letter* (1939-1945). He also founded the Moot (1938) and the Christian Frontier Council (1942).

Simon, Brian.
Simon wrote a four-volume history of the English education system from 1780-1990, including *Education and the Social Order, 1940-1990*. Simon's *History of Education, 1780-1870* symbolizes the shift to labor history interpretations of class conflicts in British education. Simon was a prolific and widely influential writer, professor of education, and educational activist. Simon was also a life-long and often radical advocate for egalitarian secondary schooling through comprehensive schooling. He served as a founder and collaborator on the Comprehensive Schools Committee and the journal *Forum*; served as education spokesman for the Communist Party in England; and as an opponent of intelligence testing and the eleven-plus exam.

Simon, Shena.
In 1911 Simon became an active secretary of a committee safeguarding women's rights under Lloyd George's insurance bill (1911). She was the founder of "The Women Citizens' Association," a local branch of the National Women Citizens' Association; Lady Mayoress of Manchester (1921); Member of Manchester City Council (1924-1933); Member of the Royal Committee on Licensing (1929); Member of Estate Council (1931-33); and the first woman to hold the office of Chairman of Education Committee (1932-33). Simon was actively involved in the Spens Report (1933). Simon joined the Labour Party in 1935. She served as Chair of the Further Education Sub-committee (194[4]-195[1]); Chair of the Workers Educational Associations' Educational Advisory Committee (1946); and Honorary Freeman of Manchester 1964. Her son was the acclaimed historian of education Brian Simon.

Tawney, Richard Henry.
Tawney was author of Labour Party reports including: *Secondary Education for All* (1922) and *Education: The Socialist Policy* (1924). He was also a collaborator on the *Christian News-Letter*.

Temple, William.
The 98th Archbishop of Canterbury Temple also wrote *Christianity and the Social Order* (1942) and *The Church Looks Forward* (1944). *Christianity and the Social Order* examined socio-cultural and socio-economic trends and made recommendations for the Church's contemporary and future role on the social order. Temple was committed to education and played an intricate role in shaping the 1944 Act and reaching a church-state compromise with President of the Board of Education, R. A. Butler. Temple was a member of the Moot and a

collaborator on the *Christian News-Letter*.

Zimmern, Alfred Eckhard.
Scholar and authority on international institutions who worked in association with Oxford and the Workers' Educational Association to produce *Oxford and Working-Class Education* (1908) which recommended extension of educational opportunities.

Terms

1988 Education Reform Act.
Under Prime Minister Margaret Thatcher and Secretary of State for Education and Science Kenneth Baker the Act established the National Curriculum 5—16. The Act changed the language of religious education policy to note that "collective worship required in the school by section 6 of this Act shall be wholly or mainly of a broadly Christian character" (7.1). The Act also stipulated: "For the purposes of subsection (1) . . . collective worship is of a broadly Christian character if it reflects the broad traditions of Christian belief without being distinctive of any particular Christian denomination," (7.2) and "[a]ny agreed syllabus which after this section comes into force is adopted or deemed to be adopted under Schedule 5 to that Act (which, as amended by this Act, provides for the preparation, adoption and reconsideration of an agreed syllabus of religious education) shall reflect the fact that the religious traditions in Great Britain are in the main Christian whilst taking account of the teaching and practices of the other principal religions represented in Great Britain" (8.3).

All Souls Group.
The All Souls Group was convened by Warden Dr. W. G. S. Adams in June 1941. The group was created specifically to address issues and problems in education during World War II and those expected in the postwar era. The group brought together a circle of leading educationalists in close contact with the President of the Board of Education, R. A. Butler, who attended meetings as a guest. Its deliberations helped shape wartime and postwar educational decisions.

Beveridge Report.
A November 1942 report by Sir William Beveridge entitled *Social Insurance and Allied Services*. It presented plans for British welfare schemes including national health insurance, unemployment insurance and old-age pensions among others.

Bipartite.
An educational system comprising selective and non-selective schools typically grammar and secondary moderns although either of these could be paired with a technical school. See also **tripartite, comprehensive, grammar school, technical school** and **modern school.**

Central Advisory Councils.
English and Welsh Councils to advise the Secretary of State on educational issues. R. A. Butler chose Fred Clarke as the chair of the first Central Advisory Council. Significant Central Advisory Council reports include the Crowther Report (1959); the Newsom Report (1963); and the Plowden Report (1967). Other reports include: "School and Life: a First Enquiry into the Transition From School to Independent Life," (1947); "Out Of School, the Second Report of the Central Advisory Council for Education," (1948); "Early Leaving; A Report;" (1954); and "The Youth Service in England and Wales," Lady Albemarle, chair, (1960).

Christian News-Letter.
The *Christian News-Letter* was established in 1939 by J. H. Oldham in connection with the Council on the Christian Faith and the Common Life. Forty-eight collaborators were listed in the first issues including The Archbishop of York (William Temple), Fred Clarke, Canon F. A. Cockin, T. S. Eliot, Karl Mannheim, Walter Moberly, Walter Oakeshott, Dorothy Sayers, Arnold Toynbee, and R. H. Tawney.

Comprehensive school.
A comprehensive school is often seen as a school or school system based on an ideal of a non-selective, common course of study for all students. A lack of agreement and consensus over the experimental versus socially-just nature of comprehensive schools in England (even among supporters) divided the comprehensive ideal between a meritocratic comprehensive principle and an egalitarian comprehensive principle.

Conservative Sub-committee on Education.
R. A. Butler created the Conservative Sub-committee on Education in 1941 both to address issues of education and to circumvent the limitations put on the Board of Education in regard to education reform by Prime Minister Winston Churchill during the tumultuous years of the World War II. Butler hand-picked Geoffrey Faber, publisher and historian, as chair of the Conservative Sub-committee on Education. The committee that formed included a variety of men and women including, but not limited to, the vice-chairman of the committee, Harold Webbe, T. F. Watson, the committee's secretary, and Walter F. Oakeshott, college head and schoolmaster. The Conservative Sub-committee on Education produced three reports all titled "Looking Ahead." The sub-titles of the reports read: *Educational Aims*, (1942); *A Plan for Youth,* (1942); and *The Statutory Educational System*, (1944). Fred Clarke, educationalist, and Karl Mannheim, sociologist influenced the content of these reports.

Consultative Committee.
The Board of Education Act created this advisory committee which issued significant reports including: Hadow (1926, 1931, and 1933) and Spens (1938), covering elements of both elementary and secondary

education. Following the 1944 Education Act two Central Advisory Councils, for England and Wales replaced the Consultative Committee.

County college.
County colleges for part-time education for 15-18 year olds were recommended in the 1943 White Paper on Educational Reconstruction. Originally envisioned to open in 1950, other postwar priorities delayed implementation of county colleges despite the 1959 Crowther Report's advice to implement this system of part-time education for school-leavers.

Dual system.
System of education in England, in which both the state and the churches provide education with the state providing subsidies to the church, or voluntary, schools in return for agreed-upon management and curriculum decisions.

Educationalist.
British-English idiom. Refers to a specialist in the theory and practice of education but is also used freely for those who work in or are activists for education.

Eleven plus examination.
Local Education Authority examinations administered to determine selective secondary schools student body.

Further education.
British-English idiom. All formal education attained after school-leaving that was mainly geared toward vocational training and often administered by Local Educational Authorities. See also **higher education**, **county college** and **youth service**.

(Secondary) Grammar school.
A secondary grammar school has generally been envisioned as one that provided courses geared toward attending a sixth form, or a level of specialized study necessary in preparation for meeting university entry requirements, such as general requirements called "A levels." Due to complex social, cultural, and historical reasons, grammar schools became associated with contentious ideals of intelligence, academic ability, high social class, and elitism. This type of school dwindled in the late twentieth century.

Great Debate.
On October 18, 1976 Prime Minister James Callaghan, (Labour), made a speech at Ruskin College, Oxford, interpreted as a critique of current educational practices and policies. Callaghan's speech opened the door for public debate on education as well as regional conferences on education in 1977 and the subsequent publication of "Education in Schools: A Consultative Document," a green paper.

Hadow Report.
"The Education of the Adolescent," 1926, report under William Hadow, chair, Consultative Committee of the Board of Education. Only partially geared toward secondary schooling, nevertheless the 1926

Hadow Report was influential in recommending a separation between primary and secondary education based on the finding of contemporary psychological evidence; the report also suggested that secondary education be available to all but that it should be geared to students based on assessments of their abilities. The Hadow Report is praised for its promotion of separating primary and secondary education for all students; it is also criticized for its recommendations that not all secondary students should attend the same type of school or receive identical forms of education and curriculum.

Local Education Authority (LEA).
LEAs replaced school boards following the 1902 Education Act. The LEAs were responsible for voluntary (church) schools and secondary and technical education. Under the 1944 Education Act, local educational authorities were responsible for providing a development plan for primary, secondary, and further education in their local based on local interests, needs, and wants to be approved by the new Minister of Education.

McNair Report.
"Teachers and Youth Leaders: Report of the Committee appointed by the President of the Board of Education to consider the Supply, Recruitment and Training of Teachers and Youth Leaders," Sir Arnold McNair, chair, 1944. R. A. Butler's colleague and educational expert Fred Clarke contributed to this report which was published in formal association with the Board of Education. The report, as part of an effort to expand further education and youth services in England after the war highlighted the socio-cultural provisions of a planned youth service, and the necessary employment of teachers and youth leaders to work in these fields as well as plans to bring secondary and further education closer to the world of juvenile employment, recreation, and leisure.

Ministry of Education.
The 1944 Education Act stipulated a Minister of Education rather than a President and changed the Board of Education to the Ministry of Education. In 1964 the Ministry changed to the Department of Education and Science (DES); in 1992 it became simply the Department for Education. In July 1995 the name was changed to the Department for Education and Employment (DfEE); in June 2001 the name changed to the Department for Education and Skills (DfES). By 2010 it returned to Department of Education.

Moot.
Christian intellectual group founded in 1938 by J. H. Oldham to discuss issues related to Christianity and the world order. Members included: Fred Clarke, Karl Mannheim, T. S. Eliot, P. Mairet, Walter Moberly, and group members corresponded with Archbishop William Temple.

Multilateral school.
A school that provides grammar, technical, and modern education, however, students were placed in different streams within the school.

Norwood Report.
"Curriculum and Examinations in Secondary Schools: Report of the Appointed by the President of the Board of Education in 1941," Cyril Norwood, chair. Norwood's committee was appointed in 1941 to examine secondary school curriculum and examinations and make proposals for changes. The Norwood Committee supported tripartite division of secondary education following the Spens Report (1938).

Office for Standards in Education (Ofsted).
Formed in 1992 by the Education (Schools) Act as a new streamed-lined office of inspection and standards for schools, Ofsted is responsible for inspecting LEAs as well as nursery, primary, and secondary schools, initial teacher training courses, sixth form colleges, further education colleges, and youth work as well as all early years' child care and education. Each inspection results in a published report. Ofsted replaced Her Majesty's Inspectorate (HMI) the former agency of schools inspection.

Public school.
British-English idiom that designates a fee-based school; Americans refer to these as private schools.

School leaving age.
British-English idiom. Refers to the legal age at which English students may leave full-time, generally compulsory, (primary and) secondary education. The 1918 Education Act set this age at 14 were it remained despite attempts to raise it in 1936, until 1947 when it was officially raised to 15 as suggested by the 1944 Education Act. The official school leaving age remained at 15 until the academic year 1972-73, when it was raised to 16. Currently, students born after September 1, 1997 must continue their education and training until age 18.

(Secondary) Modern school.
"The Hadow Report on the Education of Adolescents" (1926) divided secondary education into grammar and secondary modern schools for students between the ages of 11 and 15. Modern schools were proposed to offer a general education to the majority student population.

Sixth form.
British-English idiom. Traditionally refers to two years of optional secondary education after age 16 with studies specifically geared toward helping students prepare for university or other higher education examinations, usually the General Certificate of Education A Level(s) or Advanced Level of the General Certificate of Education (GCE). The sixth form and A Levels are also the traditional training and entrance requirements for university higher education.

Spens Report.
"Report of the Consultative Committee on Secondary Education with Special Reference to Grammar Schools and Technical High Schools," 1938, Will Spens, chair. The Spens report echoed earlier proposals for free (no fee) secondary education for all. The report recommended that secondary schooling should normally be divided up into three types, grammar, technical, and modern schools.

(Secondary) Technical school.
Although these schools did not flourish in England, the Hadow and Spens reports argued they were necessary to provide higher levels of education for students who did not plan on attending university as well as specifically students interested in careers in science, technology and industry.

Selective school.
A school which bases entry on students' examination results. Although commonly associated with selection for grammar or public schools by an eleven plus examination or an examination that proffers measurement of intelligence, selection for schools can also occur to gain entry, for example, to performing or visual arts schools.

Tripartite.
The Spens Report (1938) suggested a three-part educational system of grammar, technical, and modern schools.

Youth Service.
The 1944 Education Act proposed local education authorities provide services for students and school-leavers between the ages of 11 and 25 to supplement social and cultural involvement and education.

Additional helpful references include: Peter Gordon and Denis Lawton, 2003, *Dictionary of British Education*, (London; Portland, OR: Woburn Press), and Richard Aldrich and Peter Gordon, 1989, *Dictionary of British Educationalists*, (Routledge).

SELECTED REFERENCES

London Metropolitan Archives

"Rationalists Take a Hand." 1941. *Teachers World and Schoolmistress*, October 8.

"Religious Education in Schools." 1941. *The Times*, October 10.

Christian Education Movement. 1942. "Why Christian Education Matters: The Choice before the Nation." London County Council. c. 1920-30s.

"[Citizenship Education]." In *EO/PS/2/3*. London Metropolitan Archives.

London County Council. 1944-50. "Comprehensive Schools London Development Plan, 1944-1950." In *EO/PS/1/93*. London Metropolitan Archives.

—. 1947-50. "Comprehensive Schools—Schedules of Accommodation." In *EO/PS/1/96*. London Metropolitan Archives.

—. 1938. "Criticism of London School System Made by Board of Education." In *EO/GEN/1/68*. London Metropolitan Archives.

—. 1941. "Education after the War." In *EO/GEN/1/151* and *152*. London Metropolitan Archives.

—. 1943. "Education Bill 1943." In *EO/GEN/1/154*. London Metropolitan Archives.

—. 1943. "Educational Reconstruction B/E White Paper July 1943." In *EO/GEN/1/153*. London Metropolitan Archives.

—. "*Recruitment and Employment of Teachers 1947-1951*." In EO/STA/2/77. London Metropolitan Archives.

—. 1962. "LCC Religious Education in Primary and Secondary Schools." In *EO/PS/2/40*. London Metropolitan Archives.

—. "Lectures and Classes for Teachers Religious Knowledge Course of Lectures to London Teachers, 1919-1961." In *EO/TRA1/17*. London Metropolitan Archives.

—. 1954-68 "Personal Papers of Alderman Martin Parr Concerning Comprehensive Education Generally and the Management of Shoreditch School." In *EO/PS/1/142*. London Metropolitan Archives.

—. 1954. "Proposed Report on 'Fifty Years of LCC Education, 1904-1954' Working Papers." London Metropolitan Archives.

—. "Recruitment and Employment of Teachers (Circular 1654), 1944-46." In *EO/STA/2/76*. London Metropolitan Archives.

—. 1941. "Religious Education." In *LCC/EO/TRA/1/17*. London Metropolitan Archives, September.
—. 1941. "Religious Education," In LMA/LCC/EO/TRA/1/17, September.
—. 1944. "Religious Education Conference Agreed Syllabus Conference on Religious Education July 7-8, 1944." In *EO/PS/2/37*. London Metropolitan Archives.
—. [1926]. "Report of the Consultative Committee of the Board of Education on 'the Education of the Adolescent'." In *EO/PS/1/103*. London Metropolitan Archives.
—. 1961. "Survey on RE Following Members Questions." In *EO/PS/2/40*. London Metropolitan Archives.
—. "Training of Teachers Ministry Circulars, Etc. 1946-52." In *EO/TRA/1/35*. London Metropolitan Archives.
Mass-Observation. 1943. "Religion and the People." *Christian News-Letter*, 172. In LCC/EO/PS/2, London Metropolitan Archives.
Savage, E. G. 1942. "Religious Education: Report by Education Officer." In *LMA/LCC/EO/ 2*. London Metropolitan Archives, March.

National Archives, Kew

"Alarm Felt by Conservative Back-Benchers on the Subject of Comprehensive Schools." 1959. In *PREM 11/2644*. Kew: National Archives, March 23.
"Committee on Educational Policy: Proposals for a Drive in Education." 1958. In *PREM 11/2643*. Kew: National Archives.
"Comprehensive Reorganisation of Secondary Education and Raising of School Leaving Age: Education Bill." 1965-70. In *PREM 13/3168*. Kew: National Archives.
"Comprehensive Schools." 1955. In *ED/147/208*. Kew: National Archives.
"Consultative Committee on Research into Comprehensive Education. 1965-1966. "General Papers," "Minutes," and "Objective of Comprehensive Education." In *ED/147/828-831*. Kew: National Archives.
"Correspondence between Lady Shena Simon and Minister of Education David Eccles with a Discussion of Interest in and Problems with the Soviet Education System." 1955. In *ED 147/206*. Kew: National Archives.
"Correspondence on a Revised Education Bill and Its Provisions for Religious Education in Schools 1969-1970; 1975." In *ED 183/5*. Kew: National Archives.
"Education—Various." 1941-45. In *PREM/4/11/6*. Kew: National

Archives.
"Education after the War—Green Book Drafting Papers." 1941-44. In *ED/136*. Kew: National Archives.
"Education Bill 1970 (Bill to Give S. Of S. Power to Require L.E.A's to Submit Plans for Comprehensive Education) [*sic*]." In *ED 207/19* and *20*. Kew: National Archives, c. 1970.
"House of Lords Debate on Religious Education Background Material." 1966-67. In *ED/207/29*. Kew: National Archives, 1966-1967.
"House of Lords Debate: 'Comprehensive Education,' 10 February 1965, 'the Lord Newton: Briefing Material for Lord Snow'." 1965. In *ED 136/916*. Kew: National Archives.
"House of Lords Debate on Religious Education Background Material, 1966-1967." 1966-67. In *ED/207/29*. Kew: National Archives.
"Lack of Religious Education Taught at Stockport School, Mile End, London." 1972-74. In *ED/183/1*. Kew: National Archives.
Leeson, Spencer, Rev. Canon. Leeson to Maurice Holmes, May 5, 1941. "Religious Education in Schools—General." 1941. In *ED/136/222*. Kew: National Archives.
"Legislation: Comprehensive Education." c. 1970. In *ED 147/20*. Kew: National Archives.
"Letter for D. H. Morrell to J. Syndham, Private Secretary to Prime Minister." 1959. In *PREM 11/2643*. Kew: National Archives, January 6.
"Ministry of Education and Successors: Primary, Secondary and General Education: General Files." In *ED/147*. Kew: National Archives.
"Miss Alice Martha Bacon If the Speech of the Minister of Education About the Comprehensive School, Made to the Conservative Party Conference at Scarborough, Represents the Policy of the Government. (Question to the Prime Minister, Answered by the Lord Privy Seal)." 1952. In *ED/34/192*. Kew: National Archives.
"Mr Peart What Is the Minister's Policy with Regard to the Restriction of Comprehensive School Developments." 1954. In *ED/34/198*. Kew: National Archives.
"Religious Education in Schools—General." 1941. In *ED/136/222*. Kew: National Archives.
"Secondary Education: General, 1955." 1955. In *ED 147/206*. Kew: National Archives.
"Subseries within Ed/207 Education Act 1970." 1970. In *ED 207*. Kew: National Archives.
"Summary of Main Subjects and Questions Covered by Memorandum." 1942. In *PREM/4/11/6*. Kew: National Archives.

"Weekend Seminar at Windsor on Prospects and Problems for Religious Education in the 1970s." n.d. In *ED 158/89*. Kew: National Archives.

"Notes on Certain Aspects of the Swedish Comprehensive Experiment." c. 1965. In *ED 136/916*. Kew: National Archives.

Board of Education, et. al. "Board of Education, University Branch, and Ministry of Education, Teachers Branch: Post Second World War Emergency Recruitment and Training of Teachers, Registered Files (Re Series)." n.d. In *ED/143*. Kew: National Archives.

Butler, R. A. Butler to Prime Minister Winston Churchill, September 12. 1941. In *PREM 4/11/6*. Kew: National Archives.

—. 1941. "[Memorandum] Every Year Some 450,000 Boys and Girls leave the Elementary . . ." In *PREM/4/11/6*. Kew: National Archives.

—. 1942. "Speech by the Rt. Hon. R. A. Butler, President of the Board of Education at the NUT Annual Conference." In *PREM 4/11/6*. Kew: The National Archives.

—. 1942. "The Units of Local Educational Authority: Note by the President of the Board of Education." In *PREM/4/11/6*. Kew: National Archives.

Crosland, Anthony. 1965. "Speech [Draft] N. W. Regional Council of the Labour Party, Manchester." In *ED 136/916*. Kew: National Archives.

Wolmer, Lord and Members of Parliament. 1941. "Christian Education," In "Education Various," *PREM 4/11/6*. Kew: The National Archives.

Additional Primary Sources

Christian News-Letter. 1939-49. The Council on the Christian Faith and the Common Life.

"Citizens Growing Up: At Home, in School, and After." 1949. London: Ministry of Education, HMSO.

"Curriculum and Examinations in Secondary Schools: Report of the Appointed by the President of the Board of Education in 1941, [Norwood Report]." 1941. London: H.M.S.O.

"Duty to Youth: Social Peril of Neglect: Primate's Warning." 1943. *The Times*, July 14.

"Educating for a Free Society." 1940. *Christian News-Letter*, no. 14S, January 31.

Education Act. 1944. Great Britain: HMSO.

Education Act. 1996. http://www.legislation.gov.uk/ukpga/1996/56/contents (accessed August 13, 2015.)

"Education Problems: Need for Teachers and Buildings." *The Times* April

14, 1944.
Education Reform Act. 1988. http://www.legislation.gov.uk (accessed August 13, 2015).
"Educational Reconstruction: Presented by the President of the Board of Education to Parliament by Command of His Majesty." 1943. Board of Education. London: HMSO.
"Future of Secondary Schools: Regimentation Opposed." 1943. *The Times,* January 6.
"Home News: War Damage in London." 1945. *The Times,* December 11.
"The Industrial Charter: A Statement of Conservative Industrial Policy." 1947. Paper presented at the Blackpool Conference.
"L.C.C. And Public Schools." 1943. *The Times*, January 28.
"A Landmark in Education." 1945. *The Times*, March 31.
"London School Plan: Development Plan for Primary and Secondary Education Prepared by the London County Council under the Education Act, 1944," 1947. London County Council.
"'Looking Ahead:' Agricultural Reconstruction: Being the First Report of the Sub-committee on Agriculture." 1943. Conservative Committee on Post-War Reconstruction. Westminster: Conservative and Unionist Party Organisation.
"Looking Ahead: An Account of the Proceedings of a Meeting of the Central Council of the National Union of Conservative and Unionist Associations." 1941. Caxton Hall, Westminster.
"'Looking Ahead:' Demobilisation and Resettlement: Being the First Interim Report of the Conservative Sub-committee on Demobilisation and Resettlement." 1943. Central Committee on Post-War Reconstruction. Westminster: Conservative and Unionist Party Organisation.
"Mr Churchill on Postwar Policy: Four Years' Plan for Britain." 1943. *The Times,* March 22.
"Mr. Daniel Leopold Lipson Member's Question: If the Admission of Pupils to Aided or Maintained Secondary Schools is to Continue to be Determined by Examination after Fees are Abolished on Apr. 1, and, if so, When Does He Propose to Substitute Some Other Test than an Examination at the Age of Eleven to Decide a Child's Fitness to be Admitted to a Secondary School." 1945. In *ED 34/9.* Kew: National Archives.
"A National Faith: By a Modern Conservative." 1938. London: Faber and Faber Limited.
"Nationalism and Culture." 1944. *The Times* January 7, 1944.
"Need for 70,000 More Teachers: Speed-up Scheme Urged." 1945. *The Times,* November 19.

The New Conservatism: An Anthology of Post-War Thought: With an Introduction by the Rt. Hon. R. A. Butler, C. H., M. P. 1955. London: Conservative Political Centre.

"Religion and National Life." 1940. *The Times* February 17.

"Religious Teaching in Schools: Suggested Safeguards for New Schemes: House of Lords, Wednesday, August 4." 1943. *The Times* August 5.

"School-Leaving Age: April, 1947, Fixed: 13,000 Extra Teachers Necessary." 1945. *The Times* September.

"Slum Life in Cities." 1940. *The Times,* February 17.

"The State and Education: Mr Butler on the Need for Variety." 1944. *The Times,* January 1.

"True Christian Education: Archbishop's Appeal: Effective Training for Citizenship." 1941. *The Times,* February 13.

"The Youth Service after the War: A Report of the Youth Advisory Council Appointed by the President of the Board of Education in 1942 to Advise Him on Questions Relating to the Youth Service in England." 1943. Board of Education. London: HMSO.

"The Youth Service in England and Wales." 1960. Committee Appointed by the Minister of Education in November. London: Ministry of Education.

Alexander, W. P. 1946. *The Education Act: A Parents' Guide*. London: Phoenix House Limited.

Alington, C. A. 1942. *Christianity in England: An Historical Sketch*. Oxford University Press.

Aubrey, Edwin Ewart. 1937. "The Oxford Conference." *The Journal of Religion* 17, no. 4.

Bower, William Clayton. 1941. "Religious Education Faces the Future." *The Journal of Religion* 21, no. 4.

Brophy, Brigid. 1967. "Religious Education in State Schools." *Fabian Tract* 374. London: Fabian Society.

Burt, Cyril. *Handbook of Tests: For Use in Schools*. 1923. London: Staples Press.

—. 1927. *Mental and Scholastic Tests*. London: P. S. King and Son, Ltd.,

Butler, R. A. "The 1944 Act Seen against the Pattern of the Times." 1952. Paper presented at the Jubilee Lectures, Beveridge Hall, Senate House, University of London, Institute of Education.

—. 1971. *The Art of the Possible: The Memoirs of Lord Butler, K.G., C.H.* London: Hamish Hamilton.

—. 1949. "The Birth of a Bill." In *Parliamentary Government in Britain: A Symposium*, Herbert Morrison et. al., eds. London: The Hansard Society.

—. 1946. "Foreword." In *The Future Citizen & His Surroundings: Evidence to Sir Cyril Norwood's Committee on Curriculum and Examinations in Secondary Schools*, ed. W. F. Morris. London: B. T. Batsford, LTD.

—. 1950. "Foreword." In *The Great Betrayal: the Impact of Nationalisation on the Worker, the Trade Union, Local Authorities, the Consumer, Management & the Taxpayer since 1946*, James R. H. Hutchinson, ed. Conservative Political Center.

—. 1946. "Foreword." In *The Education Act: A Parents' Guide*. London: Phoenix House Limited.

—. 1939. "The Future of Political Education: An Address Given, as Chairman of the Central Education Committee." In *The Conference on Political Education*. Ashridge: National Union of Conservative and Unionist Associations (edition: Mikrofiche-Ausg. from Niedersaechsische Staats-und Universitaets Bibliothek Goettingen).

—. 1955. "Invest in Success." In *The New Conservatism: An Anthology of Post-War Thought*. London: Conservative Political Centre.

—. 1938. "The Issues in British Foreign Policy." *International Affairs (Royal Institute of International Affairs 1931-1939)*, no. 3 (May-June).

—. 1956. "Our Way Ahead." In *Conservative Political Centre Meeting in Connection with the Party Conference*. Llandudno, Wales: Conservative Political Centre, London.

—. 1943. "Preface." In *Forward from Victory: A Book on the Problems of Reconstruction*, edited by Four Young Conservatives. London: Faber and Faber Limited.

—. 1938. "Preface." In *A National Faith: By a Modern Conservative*. London: Faber and Faber Limited.

—. 1948. "Return to Greatness: A Statement of the Aims and Achievements of the Conservative Political Education Movement." London: Conservative Political Centre.

—. 1963. *This Is Conservative Policy*. London: Conservative & Unionist Central Office.

—. 1947. *What Do You Think? Facts and Ideas for Discussion Groups and Students: R. A. Butler Talks with You About the Industrial Charter*. London: Conservative Political Centre.

Central Advisory Council for Education. 1947. "School and Life: A First Enquiry into the Transition from School to Independent Life, Sir Fred Clarke, chair." Ministry of Education. London.

Charles, Enid. 1936. *The Menace of Underpopulation: A Biological Study of the Decline of Population Growth*, London: Watts and Company.

Chataway, Christopher. 1965. "Education and the Parent." In *The*

Conservative Opportunity: Fifteen Bow Group Essays on Tomorrow's Toryism. B. T. Batsford LTD in conjunction with the Conservative Political Centre.

Chuter Ede, James. 1987. *Labour and the Wartime Coalition: From the Diary of James Chuter Ede, 1941-1945,* ed. Kevin Jefferys. London: The Historians' Press.

Clarke, Fred. 1967. "[Appendix B]: Karl Mannheim at the Institute of Education: The Beginnings, C. 1948." In *Sir Fred Clarke: Master-Teacher, 1880-1952*, ed. Frank W. Mitchell. London: Longmans, Green and Co. LTD.

—. 1940. *Education and Social Change, an English Interpretation*. London: The Sheldon Press.

—. 1945. "Education and World Order." *International Affairs (Royal Institute of International Affairs 1944 -)* 21, no. 3 (July).

—. 1923. *Essays in the Politics of Education*. London: Oxford University Press.

—. 1948. *Freedom in the Educative Society (in Memoriam K. M.)* London: University of London Press.

—. 1938. "Part I: The Crisis in Education." In *Church, Community, and State in Relation to Education*. London: George Allen & Unwin Ltd.

—. 1945. *The Study of Education in England*: Oxford University Press, 1943.

Cole, Helen C. 1945. "The Future of Secondary Education in England." *The School Review,* 53, no. 5 (May).

Conservative Sub-committee on Education. 1942; 1942; 1944. "Looking Ahead: Educational Aims; a Plan for Youth; and the Statutory Educational System." Central Committee on Post-War Reconstruction. Westminster: Conservative and Unionist Party Organization.

Consultative Committee. 1924. "Report of the Consultative Committee on Psychological Tests of Educable Capacity and Their Possible Use in the Public Education System." Board of Education. London: HMSO.

Consultative Committee on Secondary, Education. 1938. "Report of the Consultative Committee on Secondary Education with Special Reference to Grammar Schools and Technical High Schools," ed. Will Spens. London: Board of Education: HMSO.

Council for Curriculum Reform. 1945. "The Contents of Education: Proposals for the Reform of the School Curriculum: Being the Interim Report of the Council for Curriculum Reform" J. A. Lauwerys, Chairman. University of London Press LTD., Maltham House, Bickley, Kent.

Crabb, E.W. 1966. *Religious Education for the C.S.E. Year*. Leeds: E.J.

Arnold & Son Limited.
Dalton, Hugh. 1957. *The Fateful Years: Memoirs, 1931-1945*. London: Frederick Muller, Ltd.
Dempster, J. J. B. with a foreword by Sir Fred Clarke. 1946. *Education in the Secondary Modern School*. London: The Pilot Press.
Denman, The Hon. R. D. M. P. 1935. "A Note on Education." In *Towards a National Policy: Being a National Labour Contribution*. London: Longmans, Green and Co.
Dent, H. C. 1945. "Education and the New Outlook." *Journal of Educational Sociology: Philosophies Underlying European Nationalist Groups* 18, no. 8 (April).
—. 1943. "A Landmark in English Education: A Commentary on the White Paper on Educational Reconstruction Presented to Parliament by the President of the Board of Education." University of London Press LTD.
—. 1955. "The Role of the Press in Awakening Public Interest in Education." *International Review of Education* 1, no. 3.
Department of Education and Science. 1965. "The Organisation of Secondary Education (Circular 10/65)." London, (July 12).
—. 1970. "The Organisation of Secondary Education (Circular 10/70)." London, (June 30).
Eliot, T. S. 1940. "Education in a Christian Society." *Christian News-Letter: The Supplement*, 20 (March 13).
—. 1941. *Towards a Christian Britain*. London: Faber & Faber.
Elton, Lord Godfrey. 1941. "Are You Christian? We Can't Expect to Be the Shapers of a New World Era If We Lose the Faith Which Moulded Our Own History." *The Daily Mail*. November 7.
Ette, Gordon. 1949. *For Youth Only*. London: Faber and Faber Limited.
Faber, Geoffrey. 1941. "The New Threat to Books: Imperiling a Principle of High Policy." *Times Literary Supplement*, April 19.
Frere, K. H. B. 1953. "Dual Control in the Youth Employment Service." www.blackwell-synergy.com (accessed 2008).
Garnett, James Maxwell. 1943. *The World We Mean to Make and the Part of Education Making It*. London: Faber & Faber.
Gresh, Levi D. 1940. "Britain Tackled the Youth Problem." *Journal of Educational Sociology: Sociology's Contribution to Secondary Education (U.S.)* 13, no. 6.
Gross, Feliks. 1943. "Educational Reconstruction in Europe." *American Sociological Review* 8, no. 5 (October).
Hilliard, F. H. 1962. "Restoring Morals to the Curriculum." *Daily Telegraph and Morning Post*. March 7.

Holmes, M. S. 1943. "The Service of Youth: Circular 1486 (1939)." In "The Youth Service after the War: A Report of the Youth Advisory Council Appointed by the President of the Board of Education in 1942 to Advise Him on Questions Relating to the Youth Service in England." Board of Education. London: HMSO.

Hunt, Chester L. 1948. "Religious Instruction versus Secularization: The German Experience." *Journal of Educational Sociology, 22*, no. 4.

Jacks, M. L. 1946. *Total Education: A Plea for Synthesis*. The International Library of Sociology: Founded by Karl Mannheim. London: K. Paul, Trench, Trubner.

James, E. O. 1940. *The Social Function of Religion*. London: University of London Press, LTD. (University of London, Institute of Education, Historical Textbook Collection).

Joad, C. E. M. 1945. *About Education*. London: Faber & Faber.

King, Edmund. 1959. "Comprehensive Schools in England: Their Context." *Comparative Education Review* 3, no. 2.

Liebescguetz, Hans. 1941. "The Social and Educational Background of the Nazi School System." *British Journal of Educational Psychology*.

London County Council. 1954. "The Organisation of Comprehensive Secondary Schools."

London Schoolmaster's Association. 1954. "Problems of the Comprehensive School." Sheerness, England: Walter J. Cole Ltd.

Mannheim, Karl. 1944. *Diagnosis of Our Time*. New York: Oxford University Press.

—. 1951. *Freedom, Power, and Democratic Planning*. London: Routledge.

Marsden, Christopher. 1947. "Further Education in Britain." *The Journal of Higher Education* 18, no. 7.

McNair, Sir Arnold, Chair. 1944. "Teachers and Youth Leaders: Report of the Committee Appointed by the President of the Board of Education to Consider the Supply, Recruitment and Training of Teachers and Youth Leaders." Board of Education. London: HMSO.

Ministry of Education (Great Britain). 1947. "Further Education: The Scope and Content of Its Opportunities under the Education Act, 1944." London: HMSO.

—. 1945. "Memorandum on the Building Regulations: Being the Regulations Dated March 24, 1945, Prescribing Standards for School Premises, Made under Section 10 of the Education Act, 1944." London: HMSO.

—. 1945. "The Nation's Schools: Their Plan and Purpose." Ministry of Education. London: HMSO.

—. 1947. "The New Secondary Education." London: HMSO.
—. 1945. "Youth's Opportunity: Further Education in County Colleges." London: HMSO.
—. 1945. "Education for Industry and Commerce." London.
Ministry of Labour and National Service, (Great Britain) 1945. "Government Vocational Training Scheme." London.
—. 1945. "Report of the Committee on the Juvenile Employment Service." London: HMSO.
Moreton, F. E. 1944. "Attitudes to Religion among Adolescents and Adults." *The British Journal of Education Psychology* 14.
Morris, W. F., ed. 1946. *The Future Citizen & His Surroundings: Evidence to Sir Cyril Norwood's Committee on Curriculum and Examinations in Secondary Schools*. London: B. T. Batsford, LTD.
Newsom, John with a preface by The Rt. Hon. R. A. Butler, M. P. 1948. *The Education of Girls*. London: Faber and Faber.
National Association of Labour Teachers. 1939. "Social Justice in Public Education."
Oldham, J. H. 1941. *Christian News-Letter*. The Council on the Christian Faith and the Common Life, May 14.
—. 1941. *The Church Looks Ahead; Broadcast Talks*. London: Faber & Faber.
Parker, H. M. D. 1948. "Vocational Guidance for Juveniles in the United Kingdom: The Juvenile Employment Service." *International Labour Review* 57, no. 15.
Parliamentary Debates (Commons), 5th ser., vol. 396-398.
Parliamentary Debates (Lords), 5th ser., vol. 132.
Partridge, E. H. 1943. *Freedom in Education: The Function of the Public Boarding School*. London: Faber & Faber.
Rhodes, E. C. 1939. "Juvenile Delinquency." *Journal of the Royal Statistical Society* 102, no. 3.
Simon, Brian, ed. 1963. *The Challenge of Marxism*. London: Lawrence & Wishart.
—. 1991. *Education and the Social Order: 1940-1990*. New York: St. Martin's Press.
—. 1988. "The First 100 Years; the 1944 Education Act, Reforms That Have Stood the Test of Four Decades: Brian Simon Re-Assesses One of the Great Achievements of the Wartime Coalition." *Financial Times*, February 15.
—. 1971. "Intelligence Testing and the Comprehensive School." In *Intelligence, Psychology and Education: A Marxist Critique*. London: Lawrence & Wishart.

—. 1963. "The Present Predicament." In *The Challenge of Marxism*, ed. Brian Simon. London: Lawrence & Wishart.
—. 1971. "Psychology and Education; Secondary School Selection: A Reply to the Intelligence-Testers." In *Intelligence, Psychology, and Education: A Marxist Critique*. London: Lawrence & Wishart.
—. 1957. *Psychology in the Soviet Union*. London: Routledge & Kegan Paul.
Simon, Shena B. 1972. "Fabian Research Series: The Education Act . . . 1944: Provisions and Possibilities: A Guide Prepared for the Education Committee of the Fabian Society." Nendeln/Liechtenstein: Reprinted by permission of the Fabian Society Kraus Reprint.
Simpson, James Herbert. 1936. *Sane Schooling; a Record and Criticism of School Life*. London: Faber & Faber.
Tawney, R. H. 1973. "Secondary Education for All (1922)." In *Equal Opportunity in Education: A Reader in Social Class and Educational Opportunity*, ed. Harold Silver. London: Methuen & Co Ltd.
Thompson, Joan. 1972. "Secondary Education for All: A Study of Local Education Authorities' Development Plans for Secondary Schools." In *Fabian Research Series: nos. 108-122*, Fabian Society, ed.
Toyne, A. C. 1944. *Religious Teaching in Schools: A Plea for a Revision of the Syllabus: Discussion of a Vital Question: Shall the Syllabus Deal with Biblical History and Literature, or the Christian Way of Life?* Surrey: The Religious Education Press Ltd.
Williams, Griffith. 1955. "The First Ten Years of the Ministry of Education." *British Journal of Educational Studies* 3, no. 2.
Workers' Educational Association. 1947. "Secondary Education for All: Some Problems Discussed." London.

Secondary Sources

Aldrich, Richard. 1994. "Retrospective. The Real Simon Pure: Brian Simon's Four-Volume History of Education in England." *History of Education Quarterly* 34, no. 1 (Spring).
—. 2003. "The Three Duties of the Historian of Education." *History of Education Journal* 32, no. 2.
Aldrich, Richard and Peter Gordon. 1989. *Dictionary of British Educationalists*: Routledge.
Baldwin, R. N. 1975. *The Great Comprehensive School Gamble: Statistics of Secondary School Examinations, 1966-1973*. London: Macclesfield: Helios Press.
Banks, Olive. 1958. "Social Mobility and the English System of

Education." *International Review of Education* 4, no. 2, Education and Sociology.

Barber, Michael. 1994. *The Making of the 1944 Education Act*. London and New York: Cassell.

Barnett, Correlli. 1986. *The Audit of War: The Illusion and Reality of Britain as a Great Nation* London: Macmillan.

Beales, A. C. F. 1951. "Education in England, 1939-1946." *History of Education Journal* 2, no. 3 (Spring).

Beer, Samuel. 1952. "The Conservative Party of Great Britain." *The Journal of Politics* 14, no. 1.

—. 1965. *Modern British Politics*. New York: Random House.

Benn, Caroline. 1974. "England Lags Behind." *Forum for the Discussion of New Trends in Education* 16, no. 3.

Benn, Caroline and Brian Simon. 1970. *Half Way There: Report on the British Comprehensive School Reform*: Penguin Books.

Berkowitz, Peter. 2007. "Liberal Education, Then and Now; J. S. Mill's Idea of a University, and Our Own." *Hoover Institution Policy Review* (January).

Bevir, Mark. 1997. "Labour Churches and Ethical Socialism." *History Today* 47, no. 4.

—. 2000. "Republicanism, Socialism, and Democracy in Britain: The Origins of the Radical Left." *Journal of Social History* 34, no. 2.

—. 1993. "Welfarism, Socialism and Religion: On T. H. Green and Others." *Review of Politics* 55, no. 4.

Blackburn, Sheila C. 1999. "A Very Moderate Socialist Indeed? R. H. Tawney and Minimum Wages." *Twentieth Century British History* 10, no. 2.

Brehoney, Kevin J. 2004. "Education as a 'Social Function': Sociology, and Social Theory in the Histories of Brian Simon." *History of Education* 33, no. 5.

Brick, Howard. 1992. "Optimism of the Mind: Imagining Postindustrial Society in the 1960s and 1970s." *American Quarterly* 44, no. 3 (September).

Briggs, Asa. "The Welfare State in Historical Perspective." *European Journal of Sociology* 2 (1961).

Brown, Callum G. 2001. *The Death of Christian Britain: Understanding Secularization, 1800-2000*: Routledge.

—. 2006. *Religion and Society in Twentieth-Century Britain*. Harlow, England: Pearson Longman.

Bryant, Christopher, ed. 1993. *Reclaiming the Ground. Christianity and Socialism*. London: Hodder & Stoughton.

Burgess, Keith. 1993. "Education Policy in Relation to Employment in Britain 1935-45: A Decade of 'Missed Opportunities'?" *History of Education* 22, no. 4.

Burgess, Tyrrell. 1970. *Inside Comprehensive Schools*. Department of Education and Science. London: HMSO.

Cairns, J. M. and E. Cox. 1989. *Reforming Religious Education: The Religious Clauses of the 1988 Education Reform Act*. London: Kogan Page.

Calder, Angus. 1991. *The Myth of the Blitz*. London: Pimlico Press.

—. 1969. *The People's War: Britain in 1939-45*. New York: Pantheon Press.

Cannon, Charmian. 1964. "The Influence of Religion on Educational Policy, 1902-1944." *British Journal of Educational Studies* 12, no. 2 (May).

Carpentier, Vincent. 2003. "Public Expenditure on Education and Economic Growth in the UK, 1833-2000." *History of Education* 32, no. 1.

Ceadel, Martin. 1991. "Labour as a Governing Party: Balancing Right and Left." In *Britain since 1945*, eds. Terry Gourvish and Alan O' Day. Basingstoke and London: Macmillan.

Chapman, Mark D. 2000. "Pluralism, Welfare and the 'Common Good': Three Varieties of Christian Socialism." *Public Theology*.

Chitty, Clyde. 1989. "The Evolution of the Comprehensive School and the Comprehensive System under Attack." In *Towards a New Education System: The Victory of the New Right?* London: Falmer Press.

—. 1989. *Towards a New Education System: The Victory of the New Right?* London: Falmer Press.

Collini, Stefan. 2006. *Absent Minds: Intellectuals in Britain*. Oxford University Press.

—. 1991. *Public Moralists: Political Thought and Intellectual Life in Britain, 1850-1930*. New York: Clarendon Press of Oxford University Press.

Crook, David. 2002. "Local Authorities and Comprehensivisation in England and Wales, 1944-1974." *Oxford Review of Education* 28, no. 2 (June).

Cruickshank, Marjorie. 1963. *Church and State in English Education*. London: St. Martin's Press.

Curtis, Mary E. and Robert Glaser. 1981. "Changing Conceptions of Intelligence." *Review of Research in Education*, 9.

Dean, Dennis. 1995. "Conservative Governments, 1951-64, and Their Changing Perspectives on the 1944 Education Act." *History of*

Education 24, no. 3.
Dean, D. W. 1971. "Conservatism and the National Education System 1922-40." *Journal of Contemporary History* 6, no. 2.
—. 1969. "The Difficulties of a Labour Educational Policy: The Failure of the Trevelyan Bill, 1929-31." *British Journal of Educational Studies* 17, no. 3 (October).
—. 1991. "Education for Moral Improvement, Domesticity and Social Cohesion: Expectations and Fears of the Labour Government, 1945-51." *Oxford Review of Education* 17, no. 3 (September).
—. 1970. "Problems of the Conservative Sub-committee on Education." *Journal of Educational Administration and History* III, no. 1.
Dearden, R. F. 1982. "Philosophy of Education, 1952-82." *British Journal of Educational Studies* 30, no. 1 (February).
Depaepe, Marc. 2004. "It's a Long Way To . . . An International Social History of Education: In Search of Brian Simon's Legacy in Today's Educational Historiography." *History of Education* 33, no. 5.
Department for Education and Skills. 2007. "Green Paper: Raising Expectations: Staying in Education and Training Post-16."
—. 2004. "Religious Education: The Non-Statutory National Framework." London: Qualifications and Curriculum Authority.
Dickson, Niall. 1999. "UK Politics What is the Third Way?" BBC News. http://news.bbc.co.uk/2/hi/458626.stm (accessed 2015).
Dierenfeld, Richard. 1981. "Religion Is a Must in English Schools." *The Clearing House*.
Dochuk, Gregory. 2006. "Training the Future Citizen: Culture, Religion and State Education in England, with Particular Reference to London, 1936-1951." PhD dissertation, Oxford.
E205, Course Team. 1984. "Conflict and Change in Education: A Sociological Introduction. Block 7, Education for What? Unit 29, Educational Policy and Ideology." Open University.
Education and Skills Select Committee. 2007. "Second Special Report Citizenship Education: Government Response to the Committee's Second Report of Session 2006-07," ed. House of Commons.
Epstein, Leon. 1954. "Politics of British Conservatism." *The American Political Science Review* 48, no. 1.
Fenwick, I. G. K. 1976. *The Comprehensive School 1944-1970: The Politics of Secondary School Reorganization*. London: Methuen & Co Ltd.
Fieldhouse, R. 1994. "The Labour Government's Further Education Policy, 1945-51." *History of Education* 23, no. 3.
Fielding, Steven. 1995. "The Crisis in Labour History." *Labour History*

Review 60, no. 3 (Winter).

Fogelman, Ken. 1999. "The Development of Comprehensive Secondary Schools in England and Wales." *School of Education: Occasional Papers University of Leicester Research*, no. Occasional Paper No. 1 (July).

Ford, Julienne. 1969. *Social Class and the Comprehensive School*. London: Routledge & Kegan Paul.

Fraser, Giles and William Whyte. 2005. "Comment & Analysis: Don't Hand Religion to the Right: The Secular Left Must Stop Sniping and Realise It Has Christian Allies." *The Guardian*, March 18.

Galton, Maurice. 2002. "Obituary: Brian Simon, 1915-2002." *Cambridge Journal of Education* 32, no. 2.

Gordon, Peter and Denis Lawton. 2003. *Dictionary of British Education*. London; Portland, OR: Woburn Press.

Gordon, Peter, Richard Aldrich and Dennis Dean. 1991. *Education and Policy in England in the Twentieth Century*. London: Woburn Press.

Gosden, P. H. J. H. 1976. *Education in the Second World War: A Study in Policy and Administration*. London: Methuen.

Griffiths, Jeff. 2006. "Afarthing for the Foundation: The History of the NFER." *Education Journal*, no. 98 (September).

Griggs, Clive. 1999. "A Life in History." *Labour History Review* 64, no. 3 (Winter).

Grimley, Matthew. 2003. "Civil Society and the Clerisy: Christian Elites and National Culture, C. 1930-1950." In *Civil Society in British History: Ideas, Identities, Institutions*, ed. Jose Harris. Oxford: Oxford University Press.

—. 2007. "The Religion of Englishness: Puritanism, Providentialism and 'National Character,' 1918-1945'." *Journal of British Studies* 46 (October).

Harris, Jose, ed. 2003. *Civil Society in British History: Ideas, Identities, Institutions*. Oxford: Oxford University Press.

—. 1991. "Enterprise and the Welfare State: A Comparative Perspective." In *Britain since 1945*, eds. Terry Gourvish and Alan O' Day. Basingstoke and London: Macmillan.

—. 1986. "Political Ideas and the Debate on State Welfare 1940-45." In *War and Social Change: British Society in the Second World War*, ed. Harold Smith. Manchester: Manchester University Press.

—. 1992. "Political Thought and the Welfare State 1870-1940: An Intellectual Framework for British Social Policy." *Past and Present* 135 (May).

—. 1997. *William Beveridge: A Biography*. Clarendon Press.

Haydn, Terry. 2004. "The Strange Death of the Comprehensive School in England and Wales, 1965-2002." *Research Papers in Education* 19, no. 4 (December).

Hollander, Samuel. 1968. "The Role of the State in Vocational Training: The Classical Economists' View." *Southern Economic Journal* 34, no. 4 (April).

Howard, Anthony. 1987. *RAB: The Life of R. A. Butler*. London: Jonathan Cape.

Hughes, Fred. 1992 *What Do You Mean—Christian Education?* Carlisle: The Paternoster Press.

Hughes, Fred. 2003. "Religious Education in England." University of Leipzig: http://www.uni-leipzig.de/~rp/vortraege/hughes.html (accessed 2008).

Jeffereys, Kevin. 1987. "British Politics and Social Policy during the Second World War." *The Historical Journal* 30, no. 1 (March).

—, ed. 1987. *Labour and the Wartime Coalition: From the Diary of James Chuter Ede, 1941-1945*. London: The Historians' Press.

—. 1984. "R. A. Butler, the Board of Education and the 1944 Education Act." *History*, 69.

Jenkins, Simon. 1952. "Conservatives and Comprehensives." Bow Group: Conservative Political Centre (Great Britain).

Judges, A. V. 1952. "The Late Sir Fred Clarke." *British Journal of Educational Studies* 1, no. 1 (November).

Judt, Tony. 2005. *Postwar: A History of Europe since 1945.* Penguin Press.

Kallaway, Peter. 1996. "Fred Clarke and the Politics of Vocational Education in South Africa, 1911-29." *History of Education* 25, no. 4.

Kang, Hee-Chun 1983. "Education and Equal Opportunity between the Wars." *Oxford Review of Education* 9, no. 2.

Kerckhoff, Alan, Ken Fogelman, David Crook, and David Reeder. 1996. *Going Comprehensive in England and Wales: A Study of Uneven Change*. London: The Woburn Press.

Kerckhoff, Alan C., Ken Fogelman and Jennifer Manlove. 1997. "Staying Ahead: The Middle Class and School Reform in England and Wales." *Sociology of Education* 70, no. 1 (January).

Kettler, David and Meja Volker. 1995. *Karl Mannheim and the Crisis of Liberalism: The Secret of These New Times*. New Brunswick and London: Transaction Publishers.

Kimball, Warren F. 1969. "'Beggar My Neighbor:' American and British Interim Finance Crisis, 1940-41." *The Journal of Economic History* 29, no. 4 (December).

Kirby, M. W. 1991. "The Economic Record since 1945." In *Britain since 1945*, eds. Terry Gourvish and Alan O' Day. Basingstoke and London: Macmillan.

Kneller, George F. 1970. "Education and Cultural Change." In *Basic Readings in the Sociology of Education*, ed. D. F. Swift. London: Routledge & Kegan Paul.

Knight, Christopher. 1990. *The Making of Tory Education Policy in Post-War Britain, 1950-1986*: The Sussex Press.

Krieger, Joel. 1999. *British Politics in the Global Age: Can Social Democracy Survive?* Oxford University Press.

Landau, Norma. 1988-89. "Eighteenth-Century England: Tales Historians Tell." *Eighteenth-Century Studies* 22, no. 2 (Winter).

Laqueur, Thomas. 1976. *Religion and Respectability: Sunday Schools and Working Class Culture, 1780-1850*. New Haven: Yale University Press.

Lawton, Denis. 1994. *The Tory Mind on Education, 1979-94*. London: Falmer Press.

Lawton, Denis and Peter Gordon. 2002. *A History of Western Educational Ideas*. London; Portland, Oregon: Woburn Press.

Leach, Robert. 2002. "Christian Socialism: The Historical and Contemporary Significance of Christian Socialism within the Labour Party." In *Political Studies Association: Annual Conference*. University of Aberdeen.

LeMahieu, D. L. 1988. *A Culture for Democracy: Mass Communication and the Cultivated Mind in Britain between the Wars*. New York: Oxford University Press: Clarendon Press.

Levacic, Rosaline and Alan J. Marsh. 2007. "Secondary Modern Schools: Are Their Pupils Disadvantaged?" *British Educational Research Journal*, 33, no. 2.

Levinson, Meira. 1997. "Liberalism versus Democracy? Schooling Private Citizens in the Public Square." *British Journal of Political Science*, 27.

Liebescguetz, Hans. 1941. "The Social and Educational Background of the Nazi School System." *British Journal of Educational Psychology*.

Loader, Colin. 1985. *The Intellectual Development of Karl Mannheim: Culture, Politics and Planning*. Cambridge: Cambridge University Press.

Louden, Lois. 2003. "The Conscience Section in Religious Education and Collective Worship: Conscientious Objection of Curriculum Choice?" http://www.culham.ac.uk/Res_conf/conscience_section.pdf (accessed 2008.)

Maclure, Stuart. 1990. *A History of Education in London 1870-1990*.

London: Allen Lane.
Mandler, Peter. 2006. *The English National Character: The History of an Idea from Edmund Burke to Tony Blair*. New Haven and London: Yale University Press.
Marsden, William Edward. 1987. *Unequal Educational Provision in England and Wales: The Nineteenth Century Roots*. The Woburn Press.
Martin, David. 1969. *The Religious and the Secular*. New York: Shocken Books.
Martin, Joyce and Jane Goodman. 2004. "Editorial: History of Education–Defining a Field." *History of Education Journal* 33, no. 1.
Marwick, Arthur. 1965. *The Deluge: British Society and the First World War*. London: Bodley Head.
—. 1967. "The Labour Party and the Welfare State in Britain, 1900-1948." *The American Historical Review* 73, no. 2 (December).
—. 1964."Middle Opinion in the Thirties: Planning, Progress, and Political 'Agreement'." *English Historical Review* LXXIX.
McCarthy, E. F. 1968. "The Comprehensive Myth." *Comprehensive Education (Bulletin of the Comprehensive Schools Committee)*, no. 10.
McCulloch, Gary. 1998. "Education and Economic Performance." *History of Education* 27, no. 3.
—. 1994. *Educational Reconstruction: The 1944 Education Act and the Twenty-First Century*. Ilford, Essex: The Woburn Press.
—. 2002. "Local Education Authorities and the Organisation of Secondary Education, 1943-1950." *Oxford Review of Education* 28, no. 2 & 3.
—. 1994. "*What Future for Education?* by Brian Simon; *Rethinking Radical Education: Essays in Honour of Brian Simon* by Ali Rattansi, David Reeder." *History of Education Quarterly* 34, no. 1 (Spring).
McCulloch, Gary and Colin McCaig. 2002. "Reinventing the Past: The Case of the English Tradition of Education." *British Journal of Educational Studies* 50, no. 2 (June).
McCulloch, Gary and Liz Sobell. 1994. "Towards a Social History of the Secondary Modern Schools." *History of Education* 23, no. 3.
McCulloch, Gary and Ruth Watts. 2003. "Introduction: Theory, Methodology, and the History of Education." *History of Education Journal* 32, no. 2.
McGuinness, Séamus. 2006. "Overeducation in the Labour Market." *Journal of Economic Surveys* 20, no. 3 (July).
McKibbin, Ross. 1998. *Classes and Cultures: England 1918-1951*. Oxford University Press.
Middleton, Nigel. 1972. "Lord Butler and the Education Act of 1944."

British Journal of Educational Studies 20, no. 2.
Milne, R. S. 1952. "Britain's Economic Planning Machinery." *The American Political Science Review* 46, no. 2 (June).
Mitchell, Frank W. 1967. *Sir Fred Clarke: Master-Teacher, 1880-1952*. London: Longmans, Green and Co. LTD.
Mitchell, Katharyne. 2003. "Educating the national citizen in neoliberal times: from the multicultural self to the strategic cosmopolitan," *Transactions of the Institute of British Geographers*.
Møller, John Christmas and Katherine Watson. 1944. *Education in Democracy, the Folk High Schools of Denmark*. London: Faber & Faber.
Morgan, Kenneth O. 1984. *Labour in Power, 1945-1951*. Oxford: Clarendon Press.
Morris, Jeremy. 2003. "The Strange Death of Christian Britain: Another Look at the Secularization Debate." *The Historical Journal* 46, 4.
Morris, Max and Clive Griggs. 1988. *Education, the Wasted Years?: 1973-1986*. London: Falmer Press.
Murphy, James. 1971. *Church, State and Schools in Britain, 1800-1970*. London: Routledge & K. Paul.
Nash, P. 1966. "Authority and Freedom in Education: Some Anglo-American Comparisons." *Comparative Education* 3, no. 1.
Office for Standards in Education (Ofsted). 2007. "Making Sense of Religion: A Report on Religious Education in Schools and the Impact of Locally Agreed Syllabuses." http://dera.ioe.ac.uk/11105/1/Making%20sense%20of%20religion%20 PDF%20format).pdf (accessed August, 2015).
—. 2002. "Teaching for Tolerance?" In *OFSTED Invitation Conference for Secondary Teachers of Religious Education*. University of Birmingham, March 27, 2002.
Olechnowicz, Andrzej. 2000. "Civic Leadership and Education for Democracy: The Simons and the Wythenshawe Estate." *Contemporary British History* 14.
Perkin, Harold. 1998. "Higher Education and Social Progress: A Comparative Perspective." *History of Education* 27, no. 3.
—. 1989. *The Rise of Professional Society: England since 1880*. London: Routledge.
—. 1996. *The Third Revolution: Professional Elites in the Modern World*. London: Routledge.
Peters, R. S. 1980. "Democratic Values and Educational Aims." In *Education and Values*, ed. Douglas Sloan. New York and London: Teachers College Press.

Pincus, Steve. 1998. "Neither Machiavellian Moment nor Possessive Individualism: Commercial Society and the Defenders of the English Commonwealth." *The American Historical Review* 103, no. 3 (June).

Pocock, J. G. A. 1975. *The Machiavellian Moment: Florentine Political Thought and the Atlantic Republican Tradition*. Princeton: Princeton University Press.

Reeder, David. 2002. "Obituary: Brian Simon: A Tribute." *History of Education* 31, no. 4.

Reeves, Marjorie, ed. 1999. *Christian Thinking and Social Order: Conviction Politics from the 1930s to the Present Day*. London: Cassell.

Reid, William A. 1997. "Principle and Pragmaticism in English Curriculum Making 1868-1918." *Journal of Curriculum Studies* 29, no. 6.

Remmling, Gunter W. 1975. *The Sociology of Karl Mannheim*. London: Routledge & Kegan Paul.

Richards, Colin. 2001. "Yet Another 'Crisis' in Primary Education? Anatomy of an Aborted Unpublished Enquiry 1948–1951." *British Journal of Educational Studies* 49, no. 1.

Richardson, William. 1999. "Historians and Educationalists: The History of Education as a Field of Study in Post-War England, Part I: 1945-1972." *History of Education Journal* 28, no. 1.

—. 1999. Part II: 1972-1996." 28, no. 2.

Rikowski, Glenn. 2004. "Marx and the Education of the Future." *Policy Futures in Education* 2, no. 3 & 4.

Rose, Jonathan. 2001. *The Intellectual Life of the British Working Classes*. Yale University Press.

Rose, Sonya O. 2003. *Which People's War? National Identity and Citizenship in Wartime*. Oxford University Press.

Ross, J. M., W. J. Bunton, P. Evison and T. S. Robertson. 1972. "A Critical Appraisal of Comprehensive Education." National Foundation for Educational Research in England and Wales, 1972.

Rothblatt, Sheldon. 1976. *Tradition and Change in English Liberal Education: An Essay in History and Culture*. London: Faber and Faber.

Rothenberg, Joshua. 1968. "The Legal Aspect of Religious Education in the Soviet Union." *Comparative Education Review* 12, no. 1.

Rubenstein, David and Brian Simon. 1969. *The Evolution of the Comprehensive School, 1926-1972*. London: Routledge & Kegan Paul.

Rudden, James. 1978. "Completing the London School Plan." *The Forum for the Discussion of New Trends in Education* 21, no. 1 (Fall).

Sanderson, Michael. 1991. "Social Equity and Industrial Need: A

Dilemma of English Education since 1945." In *Britain since 1945*, eds. Terry Gourvish and Alan O' Day. Basingstoke and London: Macmillan.

—. 1993. "Vocational and Liberal Education: A Historian's View." *European Journal of Education* 28, no. 2.

Schreiner, Peter. 2005. "Religious Education in Europe." In *Intereuropean Commission on Church and School*. Oslo University.

Scott, Jonathan. 2004. "What Were Commonwealth Principles?" *The Historical Journal* 47, no. 3.

Seldon, Anthony. 1991. "The Conservative Party since 1945." In *Britain since 1945*, eds. Terry Gourvish and Alan O' Day. Basingstoke and London: Macmillan.

Seldon, Anthony and Stuart Ball, eds. 1994. *Conservative Century: The Conservative Party since 1900*: Oxford University Press.

Silver, Harold, ed. 1973. *Equal Opportunity in Education: A Reader in Social Class and Educational Opportunity*. London: Methuen & Co Ltd.

—. 2003. *Higher Education and Opinion Making in Twentieth-Century England*: Routledge.

Silverman, Bertram and Murray Yanowitch. 1974. "Introduction: The Debate on the Working Class: Radical and Liberal Perspectives." In *The Worker in "Post-Industrial" Capitalism: Liberal and Radical Responses*, ed. Bertram Silverman and Murray Yanowitch. New York: The Free Press.

—, ed. 1974. *The Worker in "Post-Industrial" Capitalism: Liberal and Radical Responses*. New York: The Free Press.

Simon, Brian. 1965. *Education and the Labour Movement: 1870-1920*. London: Lawrence & Wishart.

—. 1991. *Education and the Social Order: 1940-1990*. New York: St. Martin's Press.

—. 1973. *The Evolution of the Comprehensive School, 1926-1972*. London: Routledge & K. Paul.

—. 1988. "The First 100 Years; the 1944 Education Act, Reforms That Have Stood the Test of Four Decades: Brian Simon Re-Assesses One of the Great Achievements of the Wartime Coalition." *Financial Times*, February 15.

—. 1971. *Intelligence, Psychology and Education: A Marxist Critique*. London: Lawrence and Wishart.

—. 1972. *The Radical Tradition in Education in Britain*. London: Lawrence and Wishart.

—. 1987. *The Rise of the Modern Educational System: Structural Change and Social Reproduction, 1870-1920*. Cambridge [Cambridgeshire]; New York: Cambridge University Press.

—. 1984. *The Spectre Haunting Education: Breaking School Rules*. London: Communist Party.

—. 1960. *Studies in the History of Education, 1780-1870*. London: Lawrence & Wishart.

Simon, E. D. 1926. *A City Council from Within*. London: Longman.

Smith, Harold, ed. 1986. *War and Social Change: British Society in the Second World War*. Manchester: Manchester University Press.

Smith, W. O. Lester. 1995. "Towards Co-Ordination in Great Britain: A Survey." *Annals of the American Academy of Political and Social Science* 302, "The Public School and Other Community Services" (November).

Snell, K. D. M. 1996. "The Apprenticeship System in British History: The Fragmentation of a Cultural Institution." *History of Education* 25, no. 4.

Soloway, Richard A. 1995. *Demography and Degeneration: Eugenics and the Declining Birthrate in Twentieth-Century Britain*: The University of North Carolina Press.

Sookhdeo, Patrick. 2006. "The Schools That Divide the Nation; the Muslim Debate: If We Are to Succeed in Defeating Extremism, We Must Resist the March of Naive Multiculturalism, Says One Writer." *The Evening Standard,* September 4.

Stapleton, Julia. 2005. "Citizenship versus Patriotism in Twentieth-Century England." *The Historical Journal* 48, no. 1.

Stelzer, Irwin M. 1996. "Christian Socialism in Britain." *Public Interest* (Summer).

Sternberg, Robert J. and Elena L. Grigorenko. 1999. "Myths in Psychology and Education Regarding the Gene-Environment Debate." *Teachers College Record* 100, no. 3.

Stevenson, John. 1984. *British Society, 1914-45*. London: A. Lane.

Stocks, John C. 1996. "Church and State in Britain: The Legacy of the 1870s." *History of Education* 25, no. 3.

Sutherland, Gillian. 1984. *Ability, Merit, and Measurement: Mental Testing and English Education, 1880-1914*. New York: Clarendon Press of Oxford University Press.

Sweeney, Mark. 2007. "Campaign Launches to End 'Educational Snobbery'." *http://www.theguardian.com/media/2007/aug/13/advertising.highereducation* (accessed 2015).

Swift, D. F. 1965. "Educational Psychology, Sociology and the Environment:

A Controversy at Cross-Purposes." *The British Journal of Sociology* XVI, no. 4.

Sylvester, Charles. 1999. "The Classical Idea of Leisure: Cultural Ideal of Class Prejudice?" *Leisure Sciences*, 21.

Taylor, William. 1996. "Education and the Moot." In *In History and in Education: Essays Presented to Peter Gordon*, ed. Richard Aldrich. London: Woburn Press.

Taylor, William. 1960. "Secondary Modern Examinations and Social Mobility in England." *Journal of Educational Sociology* 34, no. 1.

Thane, P. M. 1990. "The Debate on the Declining Birth-Rate in Britain: The Menace of an Aging Population." *Continuity and Change* 5, no. 2.

Thom, Deborah. 2004. "Politics and the People: Brian Simon and the Campaign against Intelligence Tests in British Schools." *History of Education* 33, no. 5.

Thomas, J. B. 2001. "The Beginnings of Educational Psychology in the Universities of England and Wales." *Educational Psychology* 16, no. 3.

Tinkler, Penny. 2001. "Youth's Opportunity? The Education Act of 1944 and Proposals for Part-Time Continuation of Education." *History of Education* 30, no. 1.

Tomlinson, J. R. G. 1991. "Comprehensive Education in England and Wales, 1944-1991." *European Journal of Education* 26, no. 2.

Towndrow, Frederick Edward. 1941. "Replanning Britain: Being a Summarized Report of the Oxford Conference of the Town and Country Planning Association, Spring, 1941."

Toye, Richard. 2004. "Churchill and Britain's Financial Dunkirk." *Twentieth Century British History* 15, no. 4.

Vasoli, Cesare. 1977. "The Machiavellian Moment: A Grand Ideological Synthesis." *The Journal of Modern History* 49 (December).

Viereck, Peter. 1978. "New Conservatism in the Age of Anxiety, Reprinted from *the Times Literary Supplement* (Sept. 17, 1954)." In *Conservatism Revisited*, ed. Peter Viereck. Westport, Connecticut: Greenwood Press, Publishers.

Wallace, R. G. 1981. "The Origins and Authorship of the 1944 Education Act." *History of Education* 10, no. 4.

Waller, Maureen. 2005. *London 1945: Life in the Debris of War*. London: John Murray.

Wasserstrom, Jeffrey N. 2007. "New Ways in History, 1966-2006." *History Workshop Journal* 64.

Weiner, Martin. 1981. *English Culture and the Decline of the Industrial Spirit, 1850-1980*: Cambridge: Cambridge University Press.

West, Anne, Audrey Hind and Hazel Pennel. 2004. "School Admissions and 'Selection' in Comprehensive Schools: Policy and Practice." *Oxford Review of Education* 30, no. 3 (September).

White, John. 1987. "The Comprehensive Ideal and the Rejection of Theory." *British Journal of Educational Studies* XXXV, no. 3.

—. 2006. *Intelligence, Destiny, and Education: the Ideological Roots of Intelligence Testing)*: Routledge.

—. 2004. "Should Religious Education Be a Compulsory School Subject?" *British Journal of Religious Education* 26, no. 2.

Whitty, Geoff. 2003. "Institute of Education Honours Former Student." Institute of Education Press Office, March 25.

—. 1997. "Social Theory and Education Policy: The Legacy of Karl Mannheim." *British Journal of Sociology of Education* 18, no. 2.

Williams, Griffith. "The First Ten Years of the Ministry of Education." *British Journal of Educational Studies* 3, no. 2 (1955).

Wilson, Francis G. 1960. "The Anatomy of Conservatives." *Ethics* 70, no. 4 (July).

Winter, J. M. 1986. *The Great War and the British People*. Basingstoke: Macmillan.

Wong, Jessie Yong Yuk. 1991. "Continuity and Change in Citizenship Education in England in the Twentieth Century." University of Liverpool, UK.

Woodroofe, Kathleen. 1968. "The Making of the Welfare State in England: A Summary of Its Origin and Development." *Journal of Social History* 1, no. 4 (Summer).

Wooldridge, Adrian. 1994. *Measuring the Mind: Education and Psychology in England, c. 1860-c. 1990.* Cambridge: Cambridge University Press.

—. 2006. "The Secret of Your Success." *Hoover Institution Policy Review* (June & July).

Working Group on 14-19 Reform. 2004. "14-19 Curriculum and Qualifications Reform Final Report of the Working Group on 14-19 Reform (Tomlinson Report)," ed. Mike Tomlinson. Department for Education and Skills, October.

INDEX